INVESTIGATING NOTIONS OF PROOF

A Study of Students' Proof Activities within the Context of a Fallibilist and Social Theory

Keir Finlow-Bates

Published by Flexibilis Oy of Tampere, Finland

ISBN: 978-952-92-6292-2

On the cover: the Isaac Newton Institute for Mathematical Sciences, Cambridge, where Andrew Wiles first presented his proof of Fermat's Last Theorem in June 1993. (The proof was subsequently shown to contain a flaw that was not fixed until September 1994.)

Mathematics is the only sphere of human endeavour in which you try to reduce the known to the unknown.

- Friedrichs

It has proved not to be intuitively clear what is intuitively clear in mathematics.

- Heyting

Preface to the First Edition

The following book was initially submitted in 1996 as an unpublished thesis for the degree of PhD at South Bank University (now London South Bank University). Other than some minor editing the text within is an unchanged version of the main body of the initial thesis, however, the final appendices containing transcripts of student classroom activities, previously published papers and South Bank University course materials have been removed. An original copy that includes all the material from the appendices can be obtained from London South Bank University Library or from the British Library through the inter-library loan system.

ABSTRACT

Although the question of what constitutes proof has been subject to extensive debate, there is general consensus that student achievement with respect to proof is disappointingly low. This book attempts to approach the problem of proof in the learning of mathematics from a different perspective to previous work, by constructing and empirically grounding a theory of proof based on the one hand on the fallible nature of mathematical knowledge as outlined by Lakatos, and on the other hand on the social nature of the practices involved in the process of proving, based on the work of Bloor, Rotman and Restivo.

The study commences by reviewing two pilot investigations conducted at the start of the project to focus the research questions, and the literature relevant to proof in mathematics education. The conclusions drawn from the reviews were threefold: firstly, a theory was required to found further empirical investigations and to clarify what constituted having notions of proof; secondly, it was decided that proof should be regarded as a process rather than a learning outcome; and finally, the traditional approach of devising progressive categories of proof for assessing students' understanding was rejected.

Then a theory of proof was constructed based on Lakatos' notion that proof consists of a thought experiment coupled with a proof-analysis - a decomposition of the conjecture into sub-conjectures and lemmas in order to afford a wider criticism of the conjecture, in accord with Lakatos' description of mathematics as quasi-empirical. The concept of proof as a form of social knowledge was then discussed in order to provide the theory with a deeper grounding.

Finally a qualitative empirical investigation was conducted as a realisation of the theory. The investigation involved transcribing and analysing the audio-tapings of a group of four first year university students as they worked on question sheets in the natural environment of their mathematics class. The theory proved useful in interpreting their proof-like activities.

CONTENTS

1 Introduction

It is assumed that possibly at the end of secondary school, and almost certainly at the end of a degree, mathematics students will have obtained an understanding of mathematical proof, even though it is rarely explicitly taught at any point in their education. All too frequently they are expected to come to an understanding ostensively, through a process of osmosis by exposure to written examples of proof after proof. As a result, many students have severe difficulties, even though in some cases they can "go through the motions" and satisfy the requirements of the examiners. For a society with an educational culture which purports to eschew rote learning without understanding, this situation is far from satisfactory.

Proof is a subject which has concerned the mathematics education community on many levels. There is general consensus in the literature that students' understanding of proof is disappointingly low, as evidenced in a number of studies across both a spectrum of ages (Coe and Ruthven, 1994; Finlow-Bates *et al.*, 1993; Finlow-Bates, 1994), and nationalities (Chazan, 1993; Schoenfeld, 1988, 1989; Balacheff, 1991; Senk, 1985). A variety of presentations and methods for improving the teaching of various types proof have been suggested, mostly consisting of examples of specific successful situations in the classroom (Movshovits-Hadar, 1988a, 1988b; Leron, 1985), or theoretical proposals which have yet to be thoroughly tested (Davis, 1993; van Dormolen, 1977). Part of the problem of proof concerns the conflicting desires of different levels of the educational establishments, in particular in the way proof is perceived by teachers at university and at school (Barnard, 1989; Pimm, 1990; Jaworski, 1990; Martin and Harel, 1989). The situation is exacerbated by a lack of clarity in the mathematical, philosophical and educational communities as to what actually constitutes proof, with a number of diverse roles being attributed to it (Hersh, 1993; Tymoczko, 1979; Bell, 1976; Lakatos, 1976; de Villiers, 1990; Reid, 1995a; Hanna, 1983, 1995, 1996).

1.1 Origin and formulation of the research problem

Although not offering a full mathematics degree, South Bank University provides a number of mathematics courses for first year undergraduates taking joint degrees in mathematics and business studies, and mathematics and accountancy. One such course is Mathematical Contexts and Strategies, a one semester unit intended to "develop confident, flexible and self-aware approaches to mathematical thinking and problem solving through the study of fundamental mathematical topics" (South Bank University, 1993). An aim of the course is to encourage students to reflect on their work and engage in justifying, explaining or proving their conjectures. This aim raises two questions:

1. What are students' current notions of the nature and role of mathematical proof?

2. How do students develop notions of proof?

Preliminary research (Finlow-Bates *et al.*, 1993), revealed that the majority of students had difficulties in understanding proof, and were often "failing to interpret [proofs] in the same manner as the teacher" (p.351). As indicated above, this was in line with other studies in this area. However, further research of a more qualitative nature (Finlow-Bates, 1994) suggested that students do have some understanding of proof. In particular, the students interviewed consistently used words relevant to some of the functions that have been attributed to proof. The preliminary studies are reviewed in greater detail in chapter 2.

Neither of the above studies relied on an explicit theory as to the nature of mathematical proof, although in the second study notions of what constituted proof were more developed. A conclusion that I have drawn from this is that in researching students' understanding of proof it would be useful to develop an underlying theory, or proof-paradigm, to provide a suitable perspective for the interpretation of results. Dawson (1969) posits a similar belief when he states, "Although the adoption of a philosophical position is not a necessity it does provide a basis for a consistent approach" (p.3). Thus the following two questions also require consideration:

3. What does it mean for students to engage in the activity of proving?

4. What is the nature of mathematical proof?

1.2 *The investigation*

The preliminary research (Finlow-Bates *et al.*, 1993; Finlow-Bates, 1994) has revealed that a qualitative study of a small group of students working on mathematical tasks offers significantly more opportunities to gain insights into how students deal with proof, compared to a large-scale quantitative survey. Discreetly audio-taping students working in a near-to-normal classroom environment is less intrusive and more revealing of their methods of working, compared to a questionnaire which requires them to personally analyse their own thought processes, and from which it is difficult to determine their level of attention and interest. Therefore the second part of this report consists of an investigation focusing on the conversations of a group of four first year undergraduates as they work on a set of problem sheets in the Mathematical Contexts and Strategies classroom. My analysis of transcriptions of their audio-taped conversations attempts to determine if and how the social interactions of the group help the students to develop proof or proof-like knowledge.

1.3 *The development of a theory of proof*

The theory of proof to be developed is based on two premises: that mathematics is quasi-empirical in nature, developing and growing through the "logic of proofs and refutations" (Lakatos, 1976, p.5), and that mathematical knowledge is social in nature (Restivo, 1992); "an anthropological phenomenon" (Bloor, 1983, p.83). These two assumptions will be used to derive a framework for the description of the role of proof in mathematics and the nature of proof-knowledge, thereby providing foundations for the interpretation of the investigation described above. The quasi-empiricist position can be described as a sceptical and fallibilist philosophy of mathematics. It asserts that we have no way of knowing what is true, or even that there is truth, in mathematics, but that we can only put forward tentative guesses or conjectures which are then to be tested. The process of testing either improves or refutes our initial conjectures. Lakatos coined the phrase "quasi-empirical" to describe deductive systems obeying the principle of retransmission of falsity, in which falsity travels from refuted basic statements up towards the hypotheses or premises. It is Lakatos' claim that the manner in which this occurs is through the process of the logic of proofs and refutations (Lakatos, 1976) which provides a rationale for my selection of his work as a philosophical basis. More recently de Villiers has used the term "quasi-empirical testing" to mean "the testing of conjectures by thought experiments, special cases, construction and measurement, etc." (de Villiers, personal communication). The clear role quasi-empiricism ascribes to proof suggests that it is a suitable philosophy to select when investigating the nature of proof in mathematics. There have, however, been some criticisms of Lakatos' (1976) work by Hanna (1996). These are discussed in chapter 5, although their relevance to the current work is shown to be minimal.

Once the quasi-empirical position is assumed it becomes necessary to examine how new conjectures are created and how procedures and protocols for testing are established. As this study investigates the development of proof-notions of students within the social situation of group work, it is my belief that the adoption of a social theory of the nature of mathematical knowledge and proof may lead to potentially more fruitful results than other theories. Hence, a second assumption will be that within mathematics "all talk is social" (Restivo, 1994, p.210). Proof then becomes a form of discourse within this social structure and is defined by its use, and the customs and traditions that surround it (Bloor, 1994, p.25).

In conclusion, to develop a theory of proof the study proceeds as follows:

1. an outline of the perceptions of proof in the mathematics and mathematics education communities is presented by a) identifying and examining those aspects of proof considered by the mathematics education community to be important and b) reviewing a number of schemas concerned with types and levels of proof;

2. a description and analysis of quasi-empiricism and work concerned with the social nature of mathematics is presented; and

3. a synthesis of the previous sections is used to derive a theory of proof suitable for examining students' notions of proof.

1.4 Delimitations of the report

The aim of this study is to examine mathematical proof from an educational viewpoint. The study is not concerned with the actual production of new mathematical proofs, or with explicit proof-analysis.

From all the philosophical orientations available, I have selected the position that mathematics advances along quasi-empirical lines and that mathematical knowledge is social in nature. If some other philosophical theory had been adopted the investigation might have been interpreted in a different manner, or more probably it might have developed and been conducted along different lines. However, the basis of my choice is that a quasi-empirical and social theory of proof constitutes a relevant and potentially fruitful perspective for the investigation of students' notions of proof.

A further reason I have for choosing to develop this theory of proof is one of personal preference. There are many defensible standpoints one can take as to the nature of mathematics and learning. Therefore, in the final instance the position selected, though rationally justifiable, will be made on the basis of the individual's personal experiences and beliefs.

It may be possible to derive some applications and teaching strategies, or develop new course materials from this study. However, the decision was made to restrict the investigation to one of an observational nature. Furthermore, the investigation focuses on a limited number of students working on a couple of mathematical topics. Therefore, as with most qualitative studies, insights and understanding were gained at the expense of statistically verified generalities. The significance of the study is discussed in the final section of this book along with implications for teaching.

Finally, it is worth noting that the Mathematical Contexts and Strategies course was unusual compared to standard mathematics lecture courses given in most British universities at the time. The teacher to student ratio in the Contexts and Strategies classroom was usually 1 to 15, contrasting starkly with the traditional condition of a lecture hall containing as many as 300 students listening to one lecturer. Furthermore, the course material was designed as a collection of worksheets, rather than a series of lecture notes. Without these fundamental differences I would not have had the opportunity to record students working and the investigation would not have been possible.

1.5 *Outline of the report*

The present chapter introduces and describes the nature of the study. In chapter 2 the two pilot studies (Finlow-Bates *et al.*, 1993, Finlow-Bates, 1994) conducted as a preliminary to this work are reviewed, and it is concluded that a sound theoretical basis is a requisite for a full study into student notions of proof. Chapter 3 identifies and discusses the aspects of proof considered important by the mathematics education community, as evidenced in the community's publications. Chapter 4 reviews some of the schemas of levels of proof and proof-understanding that have been put forward. In chapter 5 quasi-empiricism is analysed and the social nature of mathematics is examined in order to provide a philosophical basis for the study which, together with conclusions from the previous chapters, is used to produce a theory of the nature of proof. In chapter 6 the research methodology and experimental design for an investigation into students' notions of proof are presented. Chapter 7 contains excerpts from the transcriptions of the students working in the Contexts and Strategies classroom, which are analysed using the theory developed previously. Finally, chapter 8 presents a summary of the study together with the conclusions, limitations, and implications for further research.

2 A review of the preliminary research

This chapter consists of a review of two preliminary investigations conducted to examine students' notions of proof along with an evaluation of the influence of these investigations on this current study. They indicated the need for an explicit theory of proof in my research as well as providing a stimulus to the empirical direction taken. It is therefore important to remember that terms such as "proof" and "logical reasoning" were used in a naïve sense, particularly in the first study, and were usually intended to convey what Schoenfeld (1988) describes as a mathematician's definition of proof:

> For mathematicians, a "proof" is a coherent chain of argumentation in which one or more conclusions are deduced, in accord with certain well-specified rules of deduction, from two sets of "givens": (a) a set of hypotheses and (b) a set of "accepted facts", consisting of either axioms or results that are known to have been proven true. (p.157)

Although the sections entitled "Background" within the initial studies reveal an awareness that there are wider issues concerning what constitutes proof, the underlying assumptions corresponded reasonably with the above definition. Responses to the initial publications from the mathematics education community, in particular those questioning the underlying assumptions of the initial studies, were among the prompts that influenced the development and direction of this study as a whole. The theoretical development is examined in more detail in the chapters 3 through 5, whereas this chapter and chapter 6 provide further explanation into the development and design of the final empirical investigation. An alternative would have been to elaborate what constitutes proof by interlacing the initial studies with the subsequent theoretical analysis. However, my preference has been to emphasise the chronological development of the research.

The first study was conducted with the assistance of Dr. Stephen Lerman and Dr. Candia Morgan, who provided valuable criticisms of the questionnaire used in the investigation and co-authored the paper which resulted. The premises of that paper were that the level of formality and correctness within a proof were of paramount importance, and in particular that there was an attainable mathematical "concept of proof" although many unresolved philosophical questions remained.

In the second study the term "notions of proof" was introduced and there was less emphasis on formal aspects of proving, with an increased interest in students' perception of the roles of empirical examples and informal deductive proofs in mathematics. One of the results of the more open approach taken in the second study was the discovery that although students are often not capable of demonstrating explicit formal or semi-formal proof knowledge, they do in most cases exhibit a need for explanation, clarification and conviction in their mathematical work; notions that are commonly attributed to proof.

The conclusions drawn from this review are threefold: firstly the initial investigations revealed the necessity of a considered and explicit theory of proof, secondly they indicated that a qualitative approach to investigating students' notions of proof was more likely to yield insightful and fruitful results, and finally they suggested that proof should be approached as a process of learning and not as a learning outcome.

2.1 The initial survey

At the start of my research I conducted a survey of students' experience of proof in school and their assessment of a number of arguments put forward as proofs of a theorem about triangles. The aim was to provide a starting point for in-depth research of the nature of and students' notions of mathematical proof. Although at the time I believed I was adopting an essentially theory-less approach to the first study, in retrospect it is apparent that I held implicit unquestioned assumptions as to the nature of proof and what it means to understand proof. This section contains a review of this initial research, along with the conclusions drawn and comments on the influence it had on the final study.

2.1.1 Background

Although formal proof plays a prominent role in higher (degree level) mathematics (Hanna, 1989, 1983), attempts to teach the notion of proof are somewhat haphazard at all stages of British mathematics education, particularly at school level. Furinghetti & Paola (1991) describe a similar situation in Italian schools. Students are expected by their university tutors to have built up a concept of "formal proof" from examples given in the classroom, with very little or no guidance. The fact that the term "proof" has a substantially different meaning in mathematics to that in everyday life, and a perceived philosophical confusion about what proof really is (Tymoczko, 1979) are further hindrances. The student therefore faces the unenviable task of building a construction of the concept of proof to match that held by the established mathematicians who set the examinations, if they are to be able to provide the required answers. As Senk (1985) has shown, a high proportion of students fail to achieve this.

On the basis of the above analysis of the situation faced by students I conducted a pilot survey intended to examine their experiences and notions of proof through the use of a questionnaire. The sample group consisted of a class of first year undergraduate students at South Bank University, in the first semester of the Mathematical Contexts and Strategies course. The questionnaire attempted to determine what experience of proof students had had at school. Subsequently the theorem that the angles of any (Euclidean) triangle sum to 180° was put forward, and the students were asked to comment on the validity of a selection of "proofs" given to establish this theorem. In the published report I referred to the theorem as a fact, which is indicative of one of the assumptions concerning proof I initially held. However, it is partially through the examination and evaluation of such assumptions that the research reported here was developed.

2.1.2 Proof at school

The first question asked on the questionnaire was: "Whilst at school, did you ever 'prove' anything in mathematics? If your answer is yes could you give a short example of something you proved." The word "prove" was placed in quotation marks to draw attention to it, and yet leave its exact meaning purposely vague. Typical examples of theorems proved at school included a variety of trigonometric identities, such as tan x = sin x/cos x, Pythagoras' Theorem, and various theorems connected with

19

circles.

One of the answers given stood out:

> No, but I was asked to write down a proof of something, *e.g.*
> $d(\tan x)/dx = sec^2 x$

It seemed that the student read the question "did you 'prove' anything at school" to mean "did you personally 'prove' anything new", the emphasis being placed on "you" and not "prove".

That over two thirds of the students answered "No" or left this question blank indeed suggested that there was some confusion concerning the notion of proof in British school mathematics. Proofs of various theorems would have been presented at school, but possibly without their status as proofs being made explicit. This might have resulted in some students being unsure what was meant by the term "prove". Even those aware of the term might have been expressing the view indicated in the quote above, namely that their writing out a proof did not constitute "proving" a theorem.

2.1.3 A theorem about the interior angles of a triangle

The next section of the questionnaire offered six arguments purporting to prove the theorem that the angles of a Euclidean triangle sum to 180°. The students were asked to consider each argument in turn, and discuss, with reasons, whether it was a "good proof" or not. The following table categorises the comments written by the students on each proof:

Table 2.1 The classification of students' comments on six "proofs"

Proof number	Good	Not Good	Lack of understanding	Undecided /Blank
1	11	17	0	5
2	11	11	2	9
3	21	5	1	6
4	21	2	2	8
5	13	9	1	10
6	7	6	5	15

The term Lack of understanding was used to indicate that the student expressed an opinion which clearly indicated a lack of comprehension of the proof given - such as writing "I don't understand this proof". Where the decision to include a comment in the Lack of understanding column instead of in another column was difficult, the strategy of giving other columns precedence was adopted. For example when one student stated "This is not a good proof because the angles on a straight line might sum to 200°" his comment was tallied under Not Good, and not in the Lack of understanding column, because despite being unaware that two right angles equal 180° (an obvious case of lack of understanding) the student made a clear statement that he was against the proof.

2.1.4 Six "proofs" of the theorem

2.1.4.1   Proof 1

The "proof" given for the theorem involved measuring and summing the angles of a thousand triangles, and showing that the average of these sums was 180° by using a protractor. At most, this could be considered to be an empirical verification of the theorem for a number of test cases. It is not a mathematical proof.

Comments made by students indicating that this was not a good proof included:

> There are an infinite number of triangles in existence. One of these could possibly disprove this formula.

> This proof is inaccurate. For a topic such as mathematics accuracy is a key feature.

> An approximation and therefore not a definite conclusion

As can be seen above, the two reasons given for disliking proof 1 were that it was inaccurate, and that there might be an unexamined counterexample. None of the criticisms of the proof mentioned that it did not use any form of logical reasoning.

Some of the comments made by students suggesting this was a good proof were:

> It is a good proof because if you are a mathematician proving

21

something the different results that you get their difference mustn't be more than 5 or 4 points.

Yes it's right that the sum of the angles of a triangle is equal to two right angles because we can proof the angles of a triangle add up to 180°.

A good proof as he found the correct measurement.

The reasons given for liking the proof were usually unclear. In a few cases, such as the first quote, an empirical justification was given - namely that if we try enough cases, and get a low error then it is highly probable that the conjecture is correct. The statement "5 or 4 points" was possibly a reference to the convention in school science of considering an experiment successful if the estimated error is less than 5% of the result obtained.

2.1.4.2   Proof 2

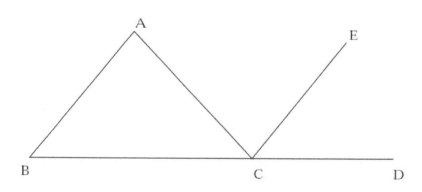

Figure 2.1 The diagram for Euclid's proof.

This proof of the theorem is that given in book 1 of Euclid's Elements. It relies on previous propositions of the equality of alternate and corresponding angles, and the construction of a line parallel to one of the triangle's sides, and passing through the remaining vertex (See figure 2.1). Comments made indicating that this proof was good included:

I approve of this method as it shows logic.

I agree with the proof as I have used its assumptions of alternate and corresponding angles when I was at school.

Most comments also included labelling the unlabelled angles of the diagram given, and writing out the algebraic sums of the angles involved with the proof. It is noteworthy that although this is a classic example of a textbook proof, only one third of the students considered it to prove the theorem.

Some of the comments made against this proof included:

Doesn't prove it. Statements don't follow and are not relevant to proof

This proof seems vague to me as it does not mention anything about the extended **BC**, nor the parallel line **CE**.

It doesn't follow from what has previously been said in the proof. If the angles in a triangle added up to 200°, everything else about the proof would still be correct except for the last line.

The most common reason for disliking the proof was due to a misunderstanding of one of the steps in the proof, by not understanding how one step led to the next, or by disagreeing with one of the initial premises. Problems arose about the extension of **BC**, and the construction of **CE**, with most of the students wanting to know why this was done.

Other problems arose with the hidden premise that the angles on a straight line sum to 180°. The convention of labelling the angle of a straight line with the symbols "180°" is usually stated as plain fact at school, without its implications on later propositions being considered. Some of the students wrote that they could see that the three angles of the triangle corresponded to three angles on the line **BCD**, centred at **C**, but for some reason failed to see that therefore the sum of these three angles must equal 180°.

The results on this part of the questionnaire verify studies by Schoenfeld who says:

... much of the mathematical knowledge that the students had at their disposal, and that they should have been able to use, went unused in problem solving. (1985, p. 13)

This statement is true for students analysing proofs as well as for those involved in problem solving.

In a couple of cases it was clear the students had failed to grasp some of the mathematical concepts required to understand the proof, for example:

> No values for the angles are given, therefore it is not possible to find the sum.

It is possible that the student cannot cope with the concept of a general triangle, or the fact that it is sometimes not necessary to know the values of variables in an equation to find their sum (*e.g. 4x - 5x + x = 0 for all x*). Another student did not understand the meaning of "Extended **BC** to **D**", and showed this by making the following comment:

> **BCD** may not be a straight line

This example was interpreted as a lack of understanding of mathematical language, rather than a lack of understanding of the mathematical concepts involved.

2.1.4.3   Proof 3

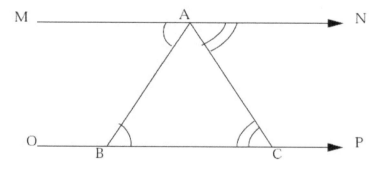

Figure 2.2 The diagram for Arnauld's proof

This proof of the theorem is that given in Book VIII of Arnauld's

Nouveaux elements de geometrie. The proof removes the assumption of corresponding angles, and relies purely on Euclid's parallel postulate and the equality of alternate angles, by constructing a triangle with two vertices on one line, and the third vertex on a parallel line (see figure 2.2). Proof 3 can be viewed as a clearer version of proof 2 (Barbin, 1992), although the perception that a proof is "clear" is obviously subjective and requires further investigation. Some of the positive comments made about this proof were:

> I feel that the proof is self-explanatory.

> This tells us about angles on a straight line, therefore it is possible to prove.

> Yes, proof works. Easy to understand. Clear.

> This proof is like the last one. (The student wrote positively about proof 2.)

The main reason for liking the proof in each case was due to the fact that it was clear, and seemed "reasonable". It is interesting to note that only two students remarked on the fact that proof 2 and proof 3 are almost identical. However, the extra clarity of proof 3 resulted in the number of positive statements made about it being double the number made about proof 2.

Some of the reasons given as to why proof 3 might be a bad proof were as follows:

> This would not convince me to believe the theorem, because nothing particular points to the actual figure of 180°.

> To prove something we have to use pure mathematic way not use shape or drawing something.

> Too abstract.

As can be seen from the comments above, the reasons for disliking proof 3 were varied. Some students disliked the proof because they could not follow its reasoning. Other students indicated that the proof was too abstract, or not abstract enough. Once again some students failed to see why the sum of the angles of a triangle should be 180°, even though the previous line of the proof convinced them that the three angles of that triangle were equal to three angles on a straight line.

2.1.4.4   Proof 4

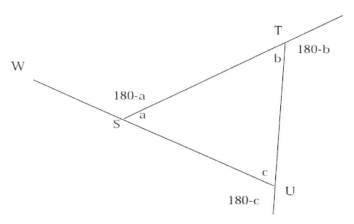

Figure 2.3 The diagram for a LOGO-style proof

This proof is based on a LOGO style of presentation, and asks the students to consider the angle a "robot" would turn through as it moves along the edges of a triangle. The proof is valid, and has the advantage of being a general proof for the sum of the interior angles of any convex polygon (see figure 2.3). Comments made in favour of the proof included:

> This gives a much clearer proof. Giving a specific formula is easier to prove.

> The logic behind [this proof] is very straightforward.

> This is very clear. I would be convinced by this proof, and it is very simple to follow.

> I think it's best way to proof because each step of proof has been explained and a person which doesn't know anything about triangle can understand the reason of $a + b + c = 180°$.

The reasons for liking proof 4 were similar to those given for proofs 2 and 3, namely that it was straightforward and logical. The fact that the workings of the proof could be reconstructed visually, by actually imagining a "robot" moving around the triangle may have helped. Finally, the proof relies on fewer, more intuitive premises, unlike the Euclidean proofs in 2 and 3 (the concepts of corresponding and alternate angles, and the construction of parallel lines are not present), and it is likely that this made the proof clearer and therefore more credible to the students (Tall, 1992, 1979).

Only two of the students disliked this proof. Their comments were:

> We do not know the angles a, b and c.

> Poor.

This proof had the smallest negative response of all the arguments given.

That almost a quarter of the students made no response or gave no decisive opinion is most likely due to the fact that it is the longest proof presented in the questionnaire – it contains at least twice as much text as any other, and some students may have been put off by this.

2.1.4.5 *Proof 5*

The theorem is demonstrated for a particular triangle, by cutting it in three, and placing the angles on a line. Although visually appealing, this does not constitute a proof, as the theorem is only tested on one triangle. Responses in favour of this proof included:

> Does not involve complex mathematical equations.

> It is easier to understand things pictorially.

As the comments show, the reasons for liking this "proof" were mainly because it was a visual, "hands-on" argument, and was very easy to understand.

Only a few of the comments indicated dissatisfaction due to the lack of generality of the demonstration:

> Good for one triangle only. Poor to assume all triangles

Most comments against the "proof" centred on the fact that using paper and scissors would not be accurate, or that it would be easy to force the corners of the triangle to fit onto a straight line, for example:

> We could say that some of this has been fiddles, *i.e.* inaccurate cuttings, adjusting parts of the cut triangles.

Proof 5 is written in "art and crafts language", referring to scissors, card, and ripping up paper triangles. This may have caused many of the students to switch out of a mathematical mode of thinking and into an every-day mode. As a result there are very few criticisms of the lack of formality or rigour of the argument given, with most comments focusing on the limitations of paper and scissors.

2.1.4.6   Proof 6

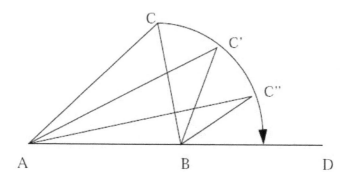

Figure 2.4 The diagram for proof 6

This argument relies on the continuous variation of a triangle. Mathematical terms, a complicated diagram (see figure 2.4), and authoritative language such as "intuitively we feel" are used to trick the reader into believing the argument constitutes a proof.

The method of continuous variation is not valid in this case, as there is no evidence that all possible triangles have been considered, and the result of 180° is obtained by calling a line segment a triangle.

A high proportion of the students gave no opinion on this argument. This is probably due to the fact that they did not feel they understood it sufficiently to write something valid, combined with the fact that it was one of the later proofs, and some of the students may have felt less enthusiastic about writing comments by this time. There is however also some evidence against this conclusion, as it was clear from notes written on the questionnaire that some of the students answered the questionnaire backwards, working from proof 6 to proof 1!

Five students actually wrote "I do not understand" or words to that effect, which was by far the highest result in the Lack of understanding column. In previous proofs many students seemed unwilling to admit that they failed to understand the arguments given, but it was seen as acceptable to confess to confusion in the case of this proof.

Seven of the students wrote comments indicating a positive attitude towards the argument. Responses included:

> Confusing but logical.

> Also a proof, but rather confusing to start off with and not as straight forward as some of the others.

> The proof is correct because it is easy to follow and is straight forward and can be done practical quickly and demonstrate easily.

The last comment was unusual for this "proof" - most comments indicated that the "proof" was very difficult to follow. It seems likely that the students had been coerced by the authoritative mathematical style used (de Villiers, 1991); in particular, the claim that the proof is "logical" has no other basis.

Six students disliked the proof. The reasons they gave included:

> Very hard to follow. Diagram is confusing, as is proof.

> Poor, using "intuitively we feel"

> This is too complicated and difficult to understand.

Only one of the comments picked up on the lack of justification for some of the steps taken in the "proof". The rest of the comments indicated that the "proof" was poor because it was hard to understand.

2.1.5 Conclusion

In *More than Formal Proof* (1989) Hanna states the following:

> The development of mathematics and the comments of practising mathematicians suggest that most mathematicians accept a new theorem where some combination of the following factors is present:
>
> 1. They understand the theorem, the concepts embodied in it, ..., and there is nothing to suggest it is not true;
>
> 2. The theorem is significant enough to have implications in one or more branches of mathematics (and is thus important and useful enough to warrant detailed study and analysis);
>
> 3. The theorem is consistent with the body of accepted mathematical results;
>
> 4. The author has an unimpeachable reputation as an expert in the subject matter of the theorem;
>
> 5. There is a convincing mathematical argument for it (rigorous or otherwise), of a type they have encountered before.
>
> (p. 21-22)

Hanna is writing about the acceptance of theorems, but she could equally have been writing about the acceptance of proofs. She goes on to say:

> If there is a rank order of criteria for admissibility, then these five criteria all rank higher than rigorous proof.
>
> (p.22)

When the comments made by the students on the proofs of the triangle theorem were examined, a surprising number of points were found in common with the way Hanna suggests the mathematical community accepts theorems. Students consistently ranked the proofs on their clarity, usefulness, consistency, how convincing they were, and how easy they were to understand before considering if they were logical and rigorous. Hanna's fourth point on reputation held as well - the arguments were all called proofs, and as a result there were only a few cases where students wrote that the argument presented was "not a proof".

By focusing on the responses of each student individually three modes of thought used to judge the "proofs" were classified, namely empirical, logical, and aesthetic. The students tended to think predominantly in one mode. Students thinking empirically favoured those arguments providing evidence supporting the triangle theorem, namely proofs 1 and 5. Students thinking logically favoured proofs providing a rational argument demonstrating the theorem from acceptable premises, namely proofs 2, 3 and 4. Students thinking aesthetically favoured proofs which they found visually or intuitively appealing, such as proofs 4 and 5. It is the logical mode of thought that is normally considered to be the most mathematical.

A closer look at the comments given on proofs 2, 3 and 4 allowed the identification of three problem areas in understanding formal proofs: failing to follow the chain of reasoning, misunderstanding a mathematical concept, and misunderstanding the language used. The term "misunderstanding" was used as a shorthand for the phrase "failing to interpret ... in the same manner as the teacher". Failure in following the chain of reasoning frequently occurred when one of the steps in the argument was considered to be "obvious" and was therefore left out. Mathematical concepts were misunderstood in several ways - examples included using axioms from an alternate mathematical frame, or failing to use previous definitions and premises (*e.g.* the case when one of the students wrote that the angles on a straight line might sum to 200°).

Failure to understand the language used occurred when a word or phrase had a specific meaning in mathematics, but is interpreted according to its everyday usage, or when the student had never encountered the word or phrase before.

2.2 The second study

The results and observations obtained from the first survey were used to develop and conduct a second investigation. The initial study was conducted without a clear methodology or theoretical foundations, and although interesting results were observed the research revealed a number of limitations. Firstly it was concerned with learning outcomes, and in keeping with other research conducted to measure the ability of students to evaluate or construct fully polished proofs with moderate to high standards of rigour, it was discovered that the students performed poorly.

Secondly, although the questionnaire used contained both specific questions and open-ended questions, it was found that the results of primary interest arose from the open questions. As a result of these observed limitations I conducted a second investigation, which showed a pronounced shift to a more explicit and qualitative research methodology with the focus on proof more as a process rather than an outcome. This section presents a review of the investigation, which consisted of the analysis of a series of video-taped interviews held to investigate first year mathematics students' notions of informal proof.

2.2.1 Background

It was concluded in the previous section that the criteria used by first year mathematics undergraduates in evaluating proof mirror those of the practising mathematician as described by Hanna (1989). However, it was found that students have difficulty applying these criteria in distinguishing empirical arguments, fallacious mathematical arguments, and proofs. Schoenfeld (1988) argues that the reason for this inability to distinguish between proof and non-proof may lie with the way proof is taught, and the aims of the student within the learning environment.

It has been claimed that in the right environment students can construct a reasoned justification for a conjecture, or even an informal proof (Hanna, 1983), but may not have the knowledge to assess, or the correct vocabulary to describe what they have produced. The aim of the second study was to investigate the value attributed by first year mathematics undergraduates to proof and examples, with particular reference to the roles they played in explaining a mathematical statement to students, and convincing them of its truth.

2.2.2 Methodology and design

As was the case with all the investigations conducted in the course of researching this book, the study was of first year mathematics students on the Mathematical Contexts and Strategies unit; a course intended to "develop confident, flexible and self-aware approaches to mathematical thinking and problem solving through the study of fundamental mathematical topics" (South Bank University, 1993). During classes students worked in small groups using a variety of worksheets. A strong emphasis was placed on the importance of working in groups rather than as individuals. The course was assessed by a course work folder containing work produced in class and at home.

During their very first class the students worked on problems concerning the closure of a variety of sets under the operations of addition and multiplication. The procedure adopted by the groups was to try a few examples to obtain an initial conjecture as to the closure of the set under the given operation. The students were then encouraged to confirm or reject this initial conjecture through the use of mathematical generalisation and justification. Proof was not formally introduced.

After the start of the course, the six participants were selected on a voluntary basis, and were interviewed separately. The interviews were designed using an adapted form of the discourse-based interview introduced by Odell & Goswami (1982) and used in an academic setting by Herrington (1985). The key features adopted from the discourse-based interview were: the interviews were based around a selection of work familiar to the interviewees, the interview was conducted in a context familiar to the interviewee, and the interviewee was assured that he/she was considered the expert. By this last feature it was hoped that the responses would be personal, rather than what the interviewee might have thought the interviewer expected.

After piloting the initial interview design on one student it became evident that the problem to be considered was too complicated. Although the few results that were obtained from this initial interview corresponded with the results of the final series of interviews they are not considered in this paper, as the initial interview was conducted as a "test-run".

The final interview design was as follows: the interviewee was given a sheet with the following question printed on it:

```
Consider the following set:
M = {x such that x is an integer greater than 4}.
Is the set closed under addition?
```

The interviewee was also presented with four solution sheets, A, B, C, and D. Solution A consisted of an informal proof similar to ones produced by some of the students in class (see figure 2.5), followed by some examples. Solution B consisted of the same examples followed by the informal proof. Solution C consisted only of an expanded version of the informal proof. Solution D consisted of examples only (see table 2.2).

```
Let y and z be in M. Let a and b be positive whole
numbers such that y = a + 4 and z = b + 4.
Then y + z = (a + 4) + (b + 4)
           = a + b + 4 + 4
           = a + b + 8
which is greater than 8 and therefore
greater than 4.
```

Figure 2.5 The informal proof included in solutions A and B

Table 2.2 The structure of the four sample solutions

Sheet A	Sheet B	Sheet C	Sheet D
Proof Examples	Examples Proof	Proof	Examples

The interviewee was told to imagine that he/she was working in a group in class on the problem, and that the four solution sheets were answers produced by different members of the group. The interviewee had the task of ranking the solutions from best to worst, to select the best solution to be included in the course work folder, explaining his/her reasons for the order selected. Then the interviewee was questioned on what he/she thought the purpose of the examples and the informal proof, in the solutions given, was. Finally, a copy of a piece of work produced by the interviewee in class was produced, and its structure was discussed in comparison to the structure of the solution selected as the best at the beginning of the interview.

All the course work produced in class on the topic of closure was collected from the participants and photo-copied. Of the five students involved in the final interview, two (R, T) had only used examples to answer questions in their course work, in a similar style to solution D in the interview. Two (S, U) had produced informal proofs followed by examples, as in solution A. The final student (V) had answered all questions in his course work using only informal proofs, as in solution C. None of the participants had produced solutions similar to solution B.

2.2.3 Results

The participants all presented an initial ordering of the solutions from best to worst, but when asked to justify their ordering during the interview all except subject T re-evaluated their ranking. Table 2.3 and table 2.4 show initial and final choices:

Table 2.3 Initial ranking of solutions

Subjects	Best	2nd best	3rd best	Worst
R	C	A	B	D
S	A	C	B	D
T	A	B	D	C
U	C	A	B	D
V	C	A	B	D

Table 2.4 Final ranking of solutions

Subjects	Best	2nd best	3rd best	Worst
R	A	B	C	D
S	A	B	C	D
T	A	B	D	C
U	A	B	C	D
V	A	B	C	D

There were three points worth noting:

1. Solution A, the informal proof followed by the examples, was consistently ranked higher than solution B, the examples followed by the informal proof. Some of the reasons for this are discussed below.

2. Solution D, consisting of examples only, was ranked worst by all interviewees except T, whose course work contained no proofs or justifications.

3. The response to solution C, the informal proof with no examples, varied the most during the interviews. Initially

ranked quite highly, solution C was later down-graded due to its lack of examples. This variation appeared to reflect student confusion about the value of proof.

The interviewees all eventually ranked A as the best solution, followed by B. The following reasons were given for preferring solution A to solution B:

> R: Because, they have, I mean, they clarify what they're doing first, and then they give some examples, of ... of the ... the solution, I mean.
> K: OK, and you think that's better than giving some examples and then clarifying?
> R: Yeah. Well, you need to understand it first, I mean, what they're doing and then the examples.

> T: So you know what you're on about, what you're on about for the examples. I believe in explaining what you're gonna do. If, when you give examples. I don't think it should be the other way around.

> U: ... I just like to have a bit of writing beforehand 'cause its explaining to me... If I look at examples before writing I wouldn't really take much notice. But if it was the other way you've read it so you want to see if it's true so you'd read it, then you take more notice of the examples.

> V: Well, I'd say A is structured better, and you can follow through much more easily what they are doing. B is basically saying the same thing, but it is not as obvious.

The reason given by all the interviewees quoted above for preferring A to B, was because A had the "explanation" before the examples, and this was considered a preferred structure for the solution. None of the interviewees referred to the initial part of A as a proof. Subjects T and U did use the word proof later on during their interview, but applied it to the examples:

> U: Yeah, because I like the way it talks about it (points at first section of A)´ and then proves it (points at second part of A), and that one (points at B) is proving, then talking about it, where I think it should be the other way.
> K: Right.
> U: That one is, it's not proving it, you know, it's just got some writing (indicating C).

> K: And the examples, what are they there for?
> T: Just to prove, prove the statement.
> K: What does that mean, "they prove the statement"?
> T: They prove, that means they make it true.
> K: So the ...

T: (interrupting) under all conditions.

I found the use of the word "proof" to describe the examples surprising, and asked subject U to explain what she meant:

K: What do you think the word "proof" means?
U: That's quite hard. Um. (Pause) I found the condition and I thought, the condition isn't just, you can't just put it down, because you're not saying if it is right or wrong. See, my proof is, like, saying if it is going to be right or wrong, that's what I think proof ... when you're proving it, you're saying that the rule is right or wrong.
K: Right, OK. So why do the examples show that the rule is right or wrong?
U: Because you're putting in, like numbers, numbers into this, and you can prove that it's right, 'cause if the answer comes out right, you know, like, if it's in the set.

U was aware that proof was connected with "saying if it is going to be right or wrong", but seemed to believe that the examples were better at this than the initial "explanation".

The interviewees had no difficulty labelling the second section of A as "examples". The first section posed more problems:

K: OK. You call the second section "examples". What would you call the first section?
V: (Pause) Erm, I'd call it an explanation of what the set is.

K: So you called these "examples". What would you call this section? (indicating second half of B)
R: The comment, you know. This? (indicating second half of B)
K: Yes.
R: What would I call this part?
K: Yes.
R: The summary of ... of ... of ... I don't know. It's just a summary.

K: What would you call this on its own? (covering the first part of B) Would you still call it a summary, or comments?
R: No, um, some notes.

The words "examples", "comments", "summary", and "notes" were all used to describe the informal proof. Although the students named the examples without hesitation, finding a phrase to label the informal proof caused the students, particularly R, some difficulty.

2.2.4 *Discussion and conclusions*

Although initially ranking informal proof on its own highly, when asked to justify their choices, students re-evaluated their ordering and selected informal proof followed by examples as the best structure for a solution to the problem. The solution consisting of examples only was considered overall to be the worst solution. Students believed the role of the informal proof to be that of explanation and clarification of the mathematical conjecture, whereas the examples were seen to fulfil the purpose of convincing them of its truth. The students had difficulty in finding suitable words to describe the section of the solution consisting of an informal proof, and the words applied to this section varied depending on its position in the overall solution.

More research needs to be carried out to determine on what basis the students made their decisions. The question remains of how the students' ideas developed, which could be determined by investigation of secondary school classrooms. Another possible influence is the structure of school mathematics textbooks, which typically introduce a topic with a piece of explanatory writing, followed by a set of exercises; this structure has parallels with solution A. The following excerpt from the transcript of subject T's interview supports this:

> T: Just to let you know how (pause), um, just to let you know how, just to let whoever's reading the book where, how the answer, how the examples make this possible.

The student changed the context of the solution here, from the situation of working in a group in class to that of a "book" aimed at an unspecified reader.

What was clear was that the students interviewed did attribute value to an informal proof as an explanation or clarification of a mathematical problem, especially as an introduction to worked examples, to the extent that this explanation is valued more highly than the examples. And yet, ironically, they seemed to be more convinced of the truth of a mathematical statement by the examples than by the informal proof. At the time of the investigation my final conclusion was that it was necessary to encourage the students to recognise the importance of proof as "an argument needed to validate a statement, an argument that may assume several different forms as long as it is convincing" (Hanna, 1989) above empirical evidence in the form of examples.

2.3 Conclusions

As was to be expected, the pilot studies had a marked influence on the design and execution of the final study. From a theoretical point of view it became apparent that a discussion about students' notions of proof was likely to be anecdotal and highly subjective without a clear theory as to the nature of proof and what it means to prove. What is noticeable in the development of the pilot studies is the shift of focus from proof as an outcome towards proof as a process. In the first study I was concerned whether students had a "concept of proof" or not, with the view that a student either did or did not know what proof was. A further assumption was that if a student had a clear "concept of proof" then he or she would have little trouble communicating this fact, given a well-designed investigation. However, by the second study I was working with the idea that students might know what the roles and functions of a proof were, and be able to identify and evaluate different proofs, without having the correct vocabulary to clearly communicate this to a researcher. I thus began to speak of student "notions of proof". From this it can be seen that the theoretical developments from the pilot studies were primarily epistemological. A final result of the studies was the decision that a more qualitative approach to data gathering and interpretation would lead to more meaningful and fruitful insights as to students' notions of proof.

3 Aspects of proof

3.1 Introduction

In the previous chapter I reviewed two preliminary investigations into first year mathematics students' notions of proof. A firm conclusion arising from these initial studies was the need for an explicit well-developed theory of proof to underpin a more in-depth study. The notion of proof involves a copious number of codes, conventions, traditions and practices, not all of which come into play in the consideration of any one proof. It would therefore seem appropriate to start the construction of a theory of proof with a review of the relevant literature. The literature was identified initially by a broad search across the fields of mathematics and education for work concerned with proof, followed by in-depth searches into areas of relevance. This approach was necessary, as mathematics education is an academic discipline without clearly defined boundaries, drawing its inspiration from such diverse fields as psychology, philosophy, sociology, mathematics and even politics. In order to gain a handle on the subject of proof I have divided my discussion into two sections. This chapter, the first part of the discussion, is concerned with the properties and attributes held in common by a great number of proofs. I have borrowed from Wheeler (1990) and Balacheff (1988) in describing these attributes as the "aspects of proof". The next chapter will consider a number of classifications schemes that have been put forward in an attempt to impose a measure on the different types of proof they identify.

Coe and Ruthven (1994) have described what I consider to be conventions relevant to proof as the "intellectual functions of proof" (p.42). They cite Bell (1976), who identifies three functions involved in the mathematical meaning of proof:

> The first is verification or justification, concerned with the truth of a proposition; the second is illumination, in that a good proof is expected to convey an insight into why the proposition is true; this does not affect the validity of the proof, but its presence in a proof is aesthetically pleaning (*sic*). The third

sense of proof is the most characteristically mathematical, that of systemisation, *i.e.* the organisation of results into a deductive system of axioms, major concepts and theorems, and minor results derived from these. (p.24)

In the next paragraph Bell identifies a further mathematical activity which he claims accounts for the production of proofs:

[Proof] grows out of the internal testing and acceptance or rejection which accompanies the development of a generalisation. (p.24)

De Villiers (1990) provides an expansion of Bell's functions of proof, with the addition of discovery and communication as further aspects, both of which are considered in greater detail in chapter 5.

Recently Hersh (1993) has argued that proof is best defined by its purposes, which he claims are primarily to convince and explain. In some cases it can be difficult or even impossible to distinguish explanation from illumination or convincing from justifying: indeed from the literature there is an indication that these terms are used in an overlapping manner. Nevertheless, providing conviction and explaining can be seen as two further aspects of proof, and are discussed in the overview below.

Finally, de Villiers (1990) points out that "although the ... functions of proof ... can be distinguished from one another, they are often intricately interlinked in specific cases. In some cases certain functions may dominate others, while in some cases certain functions may not feature at all" (p.23). For example, mathematics is often systematised through abstraction and generalisation, some explanations or illuminations can be viewed as a collection of insights, and justifications ultimately rely on a set of common beliefs often founded in intuition. As a result any categorisation will be arbitrary to some extent. In the light of the above paragraphs I have chosen to separate the aspects of proof into the following categories: abstraction, generalisation, and the generic; verification, justification and convincing; explanation and understanding; systematisation, formalisation, and axiomatisation; and finally, intuition and insight.

3.2 Abstraction, generalisation, and the generic

Two related areas of mathematics which are repeatedly associated with proof are those of generalisation and abstraction. For example, Macdonald (1978) includes them in his "metaphysical concepts associated with formal systems of mathematics" (p.411). An ability to comprehend how certain mathematical structures, such as groups or vector spaces, are abstracted from specific examples can be vital when constructing proofs of theorems within those structures. Generalisation occurs frequently within the argumentation of a proof, as for example in the construction of a valid proof by induction, which requires the ability to provide a general statement in the crucial inductive step (if $p(k)$ is true then $p(k+1)$ is true). In this section the concepts of generalisation and abstraction are considered in more detail, and the role of the generic example in proof is examined.

Harel and Tall (1991) provide the following description of generalisation:

> The term "generalization" is used both within and outside mathematics to mean the process of applying a given argument in a broader context. (p.38)

From this we can see how generalisation can be considered to be a part of proof, in that it is a technique relating to argument. Thus, if proof is regarded as "convincing argument", then generalisation can be seen as a method of proof, rather than an aim (again, for example in proof by induction). On the other hand, if generalisation is seen as an aim of proof, then a further study as to how this aim is realised is in order.

Mason (1980) considers generalisation to be one of the "key processes at the heart of mathematical thinking" (p.8). He places it in the context of specialisation and reasoning in the following manner:

> SPECIALIZATION - doing specific examples to try to find out what is meant and get a sense of what is going on.
> GENERALIZATION - trying to articulate the underlying general pattern.
> REASONING - producing an argument to verify that your articulation of the general pattern is valid.
> (p.8)

In this sense, generalisation takes place before the construction of a proof, and proof, here categorised under reasoning, involves the production of an argument validating the generalisation.

Mason and Pimm (1984) identify four words whose meanings it is important to be clear about when talking about generalisation:

> There are four words which require clarification by being compared:
> specific
> particular
> generic and
> general
> (p.280)

They proceed to illustrate how we might distinguish between "specific" and "particular" through the use of an example: the representation of an even number by the symbols $2N$. After stating that $2N$ is a shorthand for the set: $\{2N: N$ is a whole number$\}$, they present the following method of working for the mathematician:

> What seems to be going on is that the mathematician, interested in general statements which apply to a wide class of objects, avoids the semantic-philosophical difficulties, and treats $2N$ as if it were an even number. (p.282)

A few lines further down the paragraph they continue:

> Thus $2N$ is a template for identifying even numbers, a condition for admission to the ranks of the chosen. (p.282)

As a result $2N$ is sometimes regarded as a property, that of evenness, and at other times as an even object. A problem has arisen here, namely that in mathematics what is regarded as a property at one level of abstraction, may be regarded as an object at a higher level.

Mason and Pimm's (*ibid.*) final conclusion as to the difference of "particular" and "specific" is illustrated as follows:

> It seems sensible to admit $2N$ as a non-specific even number, and to emphasize the perception of it as a single, but indefinite, even number, a perception for which the word 'particular' seems appropriate. Thus $2N$ comes out as a particular, non-specific even number. (p.283)

In view of the above, the following would appear to be suitable definitions of "specific" and "particular":

- An object is specific if it is a definite, identified element selected from a class of objects. We are then concerned primarily with the unique properties of that object

- An object is particular if it is an indefinite, unidentified element from a class of objects. We are then concerned primarily with the properties of the class of which the object is a member.

Having formulated these definitions we can proceed to a consideration of the difference between the generic and the general. In simple terms, a generic proof consists of a specific example, which has all the features of a general proof relying on a non-specific particular example, and thus as long as the specific features of the generic proof are ignored it provides the same level of explanation and insight as a general proof. Mason and Pimm (*ibid.*) present us with the following generic proof of the theorem that the sum of two even numbers is even:

$$
\begin{array}{ccc}
\cdot\,\cdot\,\cdot\,\cdot\,\cdot\,\cdot\,\cdot & \cdot\,\cdot\,\cdot\,\cdot\,\cdot\,\cdot\,\cdot\,\cdot\,\cdot\,\cdot\,\cdot & \cdot\,\cdot\,\cdot\,\cdot\,\cdot\,\cdot\,\cdot\,\cdot\,\cdot\,\cdot\,\cdot\,\cdot\,\cdot\,\cdot\,\cdot\,\cdot\,\cdot \\
+ & = & \\
\cdot\,\cdot\,\cdot\,\cdot\,\cdot\,\cdot\,\cdot & \cdot\,\cdot\,\cdot\,\cdot\,\cdot\,\cdot\,\cdot\,\cdot\,\cdot\,\cdot\,\cdot & \cdot\,\cdot\,\cdot\,\cdot\,\cdot\,\cdot\,\cdot\,\cdot\,\cdot\,\cdot\,\cdot\,\cdot\,\cdot\,\cdot\,\cdot\,\cdot\,\cdot
\end{array}
$$

> It serves to remind us of an image or perception of even numbers as numbers which can be displayed as two matching rows of dots. Since in both numbers the dots pair up, so too will they in the sum, formed by amalgamating the dots. (p.284)

This is a very informal proof, and would certainly not be accepted by number theorists who would like to see such proofs embedded in a more formal theory. Even so, as Mason and Pimm state:

> The generic proof, although given in terms of a particular number, nowhere relies on any specific properties of that number. (p.284)

Unlike Mason and Pimm, who characterise the generic in terms of the particular and the general, Harel and Tall (1991) define a generic example as "a specific example seen ... as a representative of the abstract idea" (p.40), thus relating the generic to abstraction. Further on they continue: "if ... the student sees one or more specific examples as typical of a wider range of examples embodying an abstract concept, then this is a (relatively painless) form of abstraction which we call a generic abstraction." (p.40). They do admit generalisation in defining the generic, as can be seen in the following reference:

> This process [generic abstraction] clearly involves generalization (because it embeds the examples in a broader class of example embodied by the generic abstraction). But it is also a mild form of abstraction because it lifts the student's cognitive consciousness to a higher level in which the more general concept is sensed and abstracted, at least implicitly, from the generic examples. (p.40)

Understanding the distinction between abstraction and generalisation in this reference requires an examination of Harel and Tall's notion of the former. They provide us with the following description:

> An abstraction process occurs when the subject focuses attention on specific properties of a given object and then considers these properties in isolation from the original. (p.39)

When compared with their definition of generalisation quoted at the start of this section the difference, as it is perceived by Harel and Tall, becomes apparent. They consider abstraction to involve the extraction of specific properties held in common by a variety of examples, in order to construct a new abstract mathematical object, which is then considered in isolation from its origins (see also Harel and Tall, 1991, p.39), thus narrowing the focus of inquiry. Generalisation, on the other hand, is considered to involve a widening of scope in which properties or processes are seen to apply to a collection of different mathematical objects. Hence Harel and Tall consider the generic to be an abstraction, as the specificity of the generic example is ignored, and only the properties abstracted from it are considered.

To conclude, both proof (Coe and Ruthven, 1994, p.43) and generalisation (Mason, 1980, p.8) have been identified as lying at the heart of mathematics. It is therefore not surprising that the two are closely linked. Generalisation and abstraction are processes that can take place during all the phases of mathematical working, from the informal formulation and empirical investigation of hypotheses right through to the construction of formal deductive systems and proofs. It is therefore not in locating where and when generalisation takes place, or in the identification of subtle differences between the concepts of abstraction and generalisation, that the usefulness of the above research in regard to proof lies. Rather, it is in the development of a vocabulary of terms such as specific, particular and generic that the relationship of proof to generalisation and abstraction has been elucidated. Given that so many proofs rely on the particular rather than specific qualities of mathematical concepts and that most proofs are to varying extents generic in nature, an understanding of these aspects will inevitably be necessary for the production of valid proofs by students.

3.3 *Verification, justification, and convincing*

Traditionally verification, justification and providing strong convictions as to the truth of mathematical conjectures have been seen as the primary reason for proving. For example, Bell (1976) states: "The mathematical meaning of proof carries three senses. The first is verification or justification, concerned with the truth of a proposition" (p.24). As recently as 1993 Hersh has emphatically claimed that proof has one purpose in the world of mathematical research: that of providing conviction. He explicitly restates this belief seven times in his (1993) paper; three times on the first page alone:

> In mathematical research, the purpose of proof is to convince. The test of whether something is a proof is whether it convinces qualified judges. (p.389)

> a proof is just a convincing argument, as judged by competent judges. (p.389)

> In mathematical practice, in the real life of living mathematicians, proof is convincing argument, as judged by qualified judges. (p.389)

Hersh's belief in the role of proof as a means of conviction appears to be based on his experiences as a mathematician; in particular due to the fact that the pure mathematics community has as its strongest criterion for the acceptance and publication of a mathematical theorem the presentation of a proof of that theorem.

However, the acceptance of theorems and conjectures often occurs by different means. Hanna (1983) presents five criteria other than rigorous proof considered by mathematicians involved in this process:

> 1. They understand the theorem, the concepts embodied in it,

its logical antecedents, and its implications. There is nothing to suggest it is not true;

2. The theorem is significant enough to have implications in one or more branches of mathematics (and is thus important and useful enough to warrant detailed study and analysis);

3. The theorem is consistent with the body of accepted mathematical results;

4. The author has an unimpeachable reputation as an expert in the subject matter of the theorem;

5. There is a convincing mathematical argument for it (rigorous or otherwise), of a type they have encountered before.

If there is a rank order of criteria for admissibility, then these five criteria all rank higher than rigorous proof. (p. 70)

From these criteria, we can extract two factors involved in the reconsideration of the role of proof as the central means of providing conviction in mathematics. The first factor involves our practical limitations as human beings when it comes to considering a proof or set of proofs. The second concerns social and psychological issues involved in achieving conviction. Reid (1995b) supports this by pointing out that proof as the sole means of verification is flawed on two counts: "1) Proving does not always verify and 2) Methods other than proving are often used to verify theorems" (p.11).

The practical difficulties involved in using proof as a means of verification have been discussed in detail elsewhere (Hanna, 1983, p.71-74, Reid, 1995b, p.11-13). In summary, the three main concerns appear to be: the number of proofs produced every year, the unsurveyability of lengthy proofs, and the use of modern methods such as computer algorithms to prove. For examples of proofs exemplifying these concerns see Reid (1995b, p.12). The first two problems could theoretically be overcome with a suitably sized army of well-trained long-lived and dedicated mathematicians, but even if we had such an army, would we really want them to spend their time reviewing old proofs, rather than working on new ones? The third problem spans both the practical and social difficulties that can occur during verification.

Mathematics has become increasingly specialised, to the extent that, as Reid (1995b) says: "many proofs concern topics or employ techniques so abstruse as to be incomprehensible to the vast majority of mathematicians" (p.12). Unfortunately, it is not feasible for all mathematicians to learn to understand all the techniques used in proof across mathematics, but simultaneously, it is understandable that mathematicians are not, on the whole, willing to accept types of argumentation that differ from general mathematical standards.

Apart from the practicalities of proof, there are also the social and psychological aspects to be considered when examining justification, verification and convincing. Mathematicians are often convinced as to the truth of a proposition when it appears to be plausible, as suggested in Hanna's first criterion. As Reid (1995b) rhetorically asks: "Given that everyone expected Fermat's Last Theorem to be true, in what sense can Wiles' proof be said to have increased the certainty of its truth?" (p.12). Mathematicians have been so convinced of the truth of Fermat's Last Theorem that it has been called a theorem without the presence of a proof for decades. So why actually search for a proof? De Villiers (1990) suggests that:

> Proof is not necessarily a prerequisite for conviction - to the contrary, conviction is probably far more frequently a prerequisite for the finding of a proof. (p.18)

He then asks, for what other reason a mathematician would spend months or even years trying to prove a conjecture? Here the role of proof has been turned on its head, with conviction driving proof, rather than proof providing conviction. The question of how we convince ourselves and others now needs to be reconsidered. De Villiers (*ibid.*) writes:

> ... personal conviction usually depends on a combination of intuition, quasi-empirical verification and the existence of a logical (but not necessarily rigorous) proof. In fact, a very high level of conviction may sometimes be reached even in the absence of a proof. (p.18)

I would argue further, that all convictions ultimately depend on intuitive beliefs. To be convinced by a logical argument, it is necessary to believe that logical methods actually work. Similarly, to be convinced by strong empirical evidence one needs to believe in the increased probability of truth in the face of corroborating evidence. How conviction might be attained through intuitive beliefs is discussed in greater detail in the section in this chapter on insight and intuition.

De Villiers (*ibid.*) points out that it is not just the discovery of evidence for, but also the lack of evidence against a conjecture which can help us become convinced of its truth:

> Personal certainty ... also depends on the continued absence of counter-examples in the face of quasi-empirical evaluation. In the attainment of conviction, the quasi-empirical process of failed falsification therefore plays just as an important a role as the process of (deductive) justification. (p.19)

This quote also presents a clarified view of justification as an argument based on a shared set of procedures. In mathematics this is deduction using logic. Thus we can speak of intuitively held convictions being justified or verified using logical proof.

Further elements concerning the attainment of conviction are the social practices that have been built up over the years of mathematical development. Neubrand (1989), in comparing mathematical argumentation with social disputes, writes:

> At first glance, these efforts support the thesis that mathematical discussion is indeed of the same type as social discussion. One seeks for argument which can eventually be accepted, either for or against. One has to realise, however, that the word "convincing" has a decisively more precise meaning in mathematics. To be convinced depends on the high standards of argumentation which mathematicians have reached during a long historical development. (p.3)

Neubrand may well speak of "the high standards of argumentation" which have been attained in mathematics, but other communities such as parliament, the law courts, or even art critics would argue that their fields have also developed high standards. Mathematicians may rely on a more deductive style of disputing than most, but as Tymoczko, quoted in Hanna (1989), has said, "Mathematicians, even ideal mathematicians, are able to do mathematics and to know mathematics only by participating in a mathematical community" (p.22). It is a difficult and controversial task to draw critical comparisons between different cultures and communities.

I would support the argument that conviction is ultimately founded on intuitive beliefs and similarly all justifications are accepted through shared beliefs. Although verification, justification and providing conviction are all in many cases important aspects of proof, they can all take place through means other than proof. This suggests to me that they are all highly psychological in nature. The primary link between verification, justification and convincing is that they are processes involved in confirming or strengthening a belief already held, usually based on intuition. De Villiers (1991) has even explicitly used conviction, justification, verification and certainty as synonyms.

To conclude, Bell (1976) claims that:

> ... pupils will not use formal proof with appreciation of its purpose until they are aware of the public status of knowledge and the value of public verification. The most potent accelerator towards achievement of this is likely to be cooperative, research-type activity by the class. (p.25)

If students are to be taught about the "value of public verification" through proof, it is important they are aware of its limitations as well as its strengths.

3.4 Explanation and understanding

After verification, one of the most frequent aspects attributed to proof is that of explanation. Manin's (1977) frequently quoted: "a good proof is one which makes us wiser" (p.51) is evidence of this, as is the title of Bell's (1976) paper, which speaks of pupils' proof-explanations, rather than their proofs. Hersh (1993) strongly believes that whereas the primary role of proof in the mathematics community is to convince, in schools and at undergraduate level its role is to explain. He elaborates this by writing that:

> ... the purpose of proof is understanding. The choice of whether to present a proof "as is," to elaborate it, or to abbreviate it, depends on which is likeliest to increase the student's understanding of concepts, methods, applications.

> There is a difficulty in this policy. It depends on the notion of "understanding," which is neither precise nor likely to be made precise. Do we really understand what it means "to understand"? No. Can we teach so as to foster "understanding"?

> Yes. Because we can recognize understanding, even though we
> can't say precisely what it is. (p.19)

A thorough philosophical and psychological examination of what understanding might be in relation to explanation is beyond the scope of this work; however a brief discussion of some of the ideas relating to understanding and proof follows.

Hospers (1973, p.240) argues that in rational subjects such as science or mathematics providing an explanation is the same as providing a reason or set of reasons why something is believed to be true. In this sense, a proof explains if it deduces a theorem from previously accepted and understood theorems; the previously proved theorems corresponding to reasons. Bell (1976, p.28-29) reveals a similar account of proof's ability to explain in his "Categories of Response" schemes for deductive argumentation in mathematics pupils. He considers a proof to be correct and explanatory if it appeals to facts or principles which are more generally agreed on than the theorem being proved. The question of what constitutes a more generally agreed on principle remains unanswered.

De Villiers (1990), when talking about proof as a means of explanation, writes that a proof which merely provides conviction "gives no psychological satisfactory sense of illumination, *i.e.* an insight or understanding into how it is the consequence of other familiar results" (p.19). A proof which, using accepted and understood rules of inference, deduces the result from "other familiar results" and premises considered to be intuitively obvious will in all likelihood be considered an explanatory proof. As with verification, surveyability will also be an important factor, as a proof which cannot be surveyed cannot be fully understood.

Galbraith (1981), on the other hand, has taken an empirical approach by conducting clinical interviews with students in order to determine their ability to comprehend proof-explanations. Proof's explanatory role was one of the concerns of the study:

> The investigation reported in this paper was particularly
> concerned to seek insight into the understanding which pupils
> have of particular mathematical objects (concerned with
> explaining and proving), and the meanings that pupils may
> attach to forms of argument which have an agreed status in the
> mathematical world. Such understandings will be critical in
> determining what pupils regard as relevant for the purposes of

synthesizing an explanation of proof or following a reasoned argument. (p.4)

But despite Galbraith's concerns, it is difficult to extract any firm conclusions as to the role of proof as a form of explanation from his study. However, in a study along similar lines, Porteous (1990) has concluded that "proving, in the sense of explaining generalities, should be part of the normal activity of all learners of mathematics" (p.597).

Investigations into the need to explain as a form of motivation for the construction of proofs by students have been carried out. Reid (1995b), for example, has claimed that:

> Explaining provided a definite need to prove for the participants in my studies, but proving was not the only sort of reasoning motivated by a need to explain. Reasoning by analogy was also used to explain and was preferred to proving in some cases. (p.24)

Reid's separation of ways of explaining into proving and analogy provides some insight into difficulties that can occur with the use of proof for explanation. He states: "Proving is a process that must be formulated to be communicated and must be followed with some care to be understood" (p.38), whereas explaining by analogy can in some cases have an almost intuitive immediacy, and may therefore be more easily communicated.

A final complication in viewing proof as a form of explanation is that the structure of a written proof can radically change its explanatory power. Leron (1985), in discussing the rewriting of proofs relying on proof-by-contradiction, states that "better ways of presenting and communicating the products of such mathematical activities" (p.322) are necessary in the mathematics classroom. He argues that "most non-trivial proofs pivot around an act of construction - a construction of a new mathematical object" (p.323). The problem with proof by contradiction is that it involves a counter-intuitive act of destruction, and that a high level of understanding is necessary to comprehend such an act. As Leron says, "What insight do we get from a proof-by-contradiction? ... What wisdom can be derived from a contradiction?" (p.323). It is worth pointing out that this view is not in opposition to Movshovits-Hadar 's (1988b) account of the value of unexpected discovery in mathematics. Both Leron and Movshovits-Hadar are calling for mathematics to be an act of creation rather than destruction at school level, as they believe that this furthers understanding. They are also concerned with the audience that proof is to communicate with. Recognising the importance of this audience, Leron (1983) has adjusted Manin's (1977) oft-quoted aphorism to read: "A good presentation of a proof is one which makes the listener (or reader) wiser" (p.185).

In summary, the need to explain can provide a need to prove, especially in students. However, proving is not always conducted to explain; for example in the mathematics research community a proof is usually only important as an explanation to those mathematicians working in the same area, whereas the rest of the community will rely on the proof primarily as a verification. Also, explanation can take place through other means, such as explanation by analogy.

Secondly, it appears that proof as a form of explanation relies on the use of previously accepted principles, facts and methods of inference in the deduction of new concepts. In some sense the internalised and often intuitive understanding of the initial concepts carries over onto these new concepts. A proof is therefore unlikely to explain if the following three conditions are not met:

- The proof must be surveyable.

- The proof must not rely on counter-intuitive methods of deduction, unless these methods are well understood by the reader.

- The proof should only rely on a limited number of surprising insights to convey its meaning, or should have a careful, linear structure.

Thus proofs that are very long, rely on unfamiliar principles, or prove the conjecture along a surprising or convoluted line of reasoning are unlikely to have much explanatory power.

Finally, the ability of proofs to explain can be enhanced if the proofs are tailored to match the abilities of the audience with which the proofs are to communicate. This does not necessarily involve an over-simplification of the proofs, but rather ensuring that the methods and facts used in the process of the proofs are relatively well understood.

3.5 Systematisation, formalisation, and axiomatisation

Bell (1976) described the third meaning of proof to be systematisation, by which he meant "the organisation of results into a deductive system of axioms, major concepts and theorems, and minor results derived from these." (p.24). When questioning the practising mathematician it is this aspect of proof that is usually held up as its defining feature, to the extent that by "proof" many mathematicians claim to mean "formal proof" (Davis and Hersh, 1981). As Schoenfeld (1988) writes:

> For mathematicians, a "proof" is a coherent chain of argumentation in which one or more conclusions are deduced, in accord with certain well-specified rules of deduction, from two sets of "givens": (a) a set of hypotheses and (b) a set of "accepted facts", consisting of either axioms or results that are known to have been proven true. (p.157)

In comparison it is worth considering Hanna's (1983) definition of formal proof:

> The term rigorous proof or formal proof ... is understood here to mean a proof in mathematics or logic which satisfies two conditions of explicitness. First, every definition, assumption, and rule of inference appealed to in the proof has been, or could be, explicitly stated; in other words, the proof is carried out within the frame of reference of a specific known axiomatic system. Second, every step in the chain of deductions which constitutes the proof is set out explicitly. (p.3)

A problem arising from the above definition is that knowing what constitutes proof is a requirement for understanding what formal proof is. That is to say, Hanna's definition defines "formal", but not "proof". It is only in the final sentence, where formal proof is implicitly defined as consisting of a chain of deductions, that we are given some indication of the structure of a proof when it is formal. The more explicit the deductive system within which the proof resides and the more formal the proof and more formalised the theory, the higher the supposed value assigned to the proof by mathematicians of the type described by Schoenfeld.

One of the appeals of constructing an axiomatic system to describe an area of mathematics and producing formal proofs using it, is that it appears that there are no social elements in its methodology, and hence none of the subjectivity or ambiguity that such elements carry. However, the social domain does enter, in that socially determined values are used to decide on which conventions to use when selecting and working in such forms of mathematics. Consider, for example, the proposition that for any plane triangle the interior angles sum to 180°. On the one hand, we could adopt the deductive system known as Euclidean geometry to prove this statement. On the other hand we could adopt a formal system containing no rules of inference, and one axiom which states that "the sum of the interior angles of any triangle is 180°. In the second system the proof of our theorem is much simpler, but no serious mathematician would put forward such a proof for consideration by the mathematics community. And yet, there is no formal criterion why one deductive system is preferred to the another. Similarly, we cannot assert the strength of the first over the second by any means other than social ones: Euclidean geometry has a longer history and a stronger tradition, and mathematicians are merely expressing this fact when they claim that Euclidean geometry is "more interesting" than the second kind of geometry outlined.

There is also a danger in excessive formalism, namely that it reduces mathematics to the level of meaningless symbol pushing (Hanna, 1989). Rather than initially constructing a coherent chain of argumentation, the first action of an experienced mathematician when presented with a formal proof or theorem is to break it up into intuitive parts, moving to and from rigorous and theoretical approaches as and when appropriate. In Hanna's words:

> Experienced mathematicians have learned to handle this danger by acquiring the ability to make mental shifts in moving among levels of generality and formalism, and by building on specific examples, drawing only upon those characteristics pertinent to the more general situation under study. (p.23)

High standards of rigour and formality are often held up as the ideal manner in which to practice mathematics. However as Beaulieu (1990) has shown, even reputedly stringent formalists such as the Bourbaki group have used formal proofs "as a spark in the search for better settings" (p.42); that is, proofs have acted as a mechanism for the refinement and development of their systems of mathematics as much as forming the bricks and mortar of such systems, and there is more fluidity in the construction of axiomatic systems of mathematics than is usually admitted by formalists.

Systemisation is not only seen as a method of providing justification and conviction through formalisation, or as a measure of the level of generalisation present within an area of mathematics. Coe and Ruthven (1994), in considering the role of proof as a method of systematisation, have related it to understanding and clarification, stating that:

> The third function of proof is to exhibit the logical structure of ideas and to make deductive chains of reasoning explicit. This systematising function is closely related to [making sense of a result]: most theories of leaning mathematics would say that understanding consists precisely of such connections between ideas.

> However, the difference lies in the fact that logical structure is concerned with formal, explicit arguments, publicly agreed and conforming to standard conventions, while understanding is much more personal, implicit and imprecise in its connections. (p.42)

In their view of systemisation as a means of clarification, Coe and Ruthven are supported by Hanna (1989) when she writes:

> Formalism should not be seen as a side issue, but as an important tool for clarification, validation and understanding. When a need for justification is felt, and when this need can be met with an appropriate degree of rigour, learning will be greatly enhanced. (p.23)

Nagel and Newman (1959) present the following reason as to how a formal deductive system can help to clarify or explain an area of mathematics:

> Formalisation is a difficult and tricky business, but it serves a valuable purpose. It reveals structure and function in naked clarity, as does a cut-away working model of a machine. (p.27)

Carrying Nagel and Newman's analogy further, it is important that the students have an initial understanding of the area of mathematics they are studying before dealing with a formalisation thereof, much as examining a cut-away working model of a machine is unlikely to increase understanding without knowing the purpose of the machine in the first place.

To conclude, as Moore (1990) has claimed, the concepts and notions that have arisen due to the exploration of formal systems and formal proof still have a place within the teaching of mathematics :

> During the 20th century the notion of formal proof has been one of the most fertile and important notions in mathematical logic. The distinction between syntactic and semantic notions (for example, proof *vs.* truth, consistency *vs.* satisfiability, theorem *vs.* logical consequence) is something that everyone well educated in mathematics should be aware of. While educators can reasonably differ as to when students should learn these notions, they can hardly deny the fact that students of mathematics should understand formal proof - its uses and its limitations. (p.57)

Provided it is not presented as the sole ideal approach to mathematics, formalism and formal proof have a place in the education of mathematics students.

3.6 Intuition and insight

A critical in-depth investigation of mathematical intuition and insight is beyond the scope of this study. As a result I shall be relying mainly on Fischbein's (1987, 1982) and Griffiths' (1971,1978) work within this area. Intuition is relevant to proof in that, like proof, it can provide us with strong convictions or beliefs concerning the truth of mathematical propositions. There is however an inherent dichotomy within the relationship between intuition and proof in that although many of the fundamental assumptions and rules used in the construction of proofs rely on intuitive understanding, intuition can in some cases remove the desire to search for them. As Fischbein *et al.* (1981) suggest: "Accepting intuitively a certain solution or a certain interpretation means to accept it directly without (or prior to) resorting explicitly to a detailed justification." (p.491). Ensuring that student's intuitions are "prior to a detailed justification" is therefore an important part of any approach to the teaching of proof.

Fischbein (1987) points out that because "intuition is generally seen as a primary phenomenon which may be described but which is not reducible to more elementary components" (p. ix), it is often believed that a rational examination of intuition is not possible. To counter this belief he presents a functional theory of mathematical and scientific intuition. Cobb (1989) summarises some of Fischbein's main beliefs as follows:

> Intuitions are ... theories or coherent systems of beliefs expressed in terms of particular models.
>
> ...[I]ntuitions are adaptive in that they create the appearance of certitude without which practical and intellectual behavior would be impossible.
>
> Their function is to construct apparently self-evident interpretations that are essential to productive reasoning. (p.213)

Otte (1990) classifies Fischbein's approach to intuition as "essentially a Cartesian attitude" (p.37). This is mainly due to Fischbein's standpoint that "the intuitive and the analytical forms of knowledge are complementary and deeply interrelated" (Fischbein, 1982, p.11). It can be argued that Fischbein sees intuition as part of a collection of forms of knowledge spanning from perception to derived analytical knowledge. Paraphrasing (*ibid.*, 1982, p.11):

- Perception directly reflects objects or events with all their concrete qualities.

- Intuition is an immediate predominantly unconscious interpretation or derived form of knowledge which does not require the subject to provide extrinsic justification.

- Analytical or logical knowledge is a discursive consciously constructed and justified form of knowledge.

Otte (1990, p.40-41) differentiates between intuitive and analytical knowledge on the basis of time, claiming that intuitive knowledge is gained suddenly in a transfer from one mental state to another, whereas once analytical knowledge is gained it is seen as completely resolved and timeless. This is not a useful distinction from a Lakatosian viewpoint of mathematics, in which the basis for argument and hence the validity of logically deduced knowledge can change at any moment through the discovery of a counter-example, thereby removing the timelessness of analytical arguments.

But what then is the difference between intuition and insight? Macdonald (1978) presents insight as a sophisticated form of intuition, and then argues that insight is provided mainly through the examination of abstractions; in particular abstracted models. For an alternative consideration it is useful to turn to Griffiths (1978), who responds to Macdonald's (*ibid.*, p.416) challenge to provide a definition of insight as follows:

> 3. As a point of reference, let us here record the definitions given by the Concise Oxford Dictionary, as a guide to the way in which colleagues are likely to use the words:
>
> insight = 'penetration (into character, circumstances, etc.) with the understanding';
>
> intuition = 'immediate apprehension by the mind without reasoning; immediate apprehension by sense; immediate insight'.
>
> In mathematical work, these appear to manifest themselves as follows. After varying degrees of experience of special examples, skills, etc. in mathematical work, one is led to make mathematical conjectures, so:
>
> (i) intuition allows us to see that something may be (or is) so;
>
> (ii) insight allows us to see why it is so.
> (p.422)

Thus it appears that a clear understanding of the strengths and the limitations of intuition is necessary to see that a conjecture requires a proof, whereas a high level of mathematical insight is required to see how to set about proving that conjecture. In this sense, insight lies between the intuitive and the analytic.

Unlike Griffiths, Fischbein (1982) identifies two different types intuition related to two different types of proof. The types of proof are empirical proof (such as legal proof in the law courts, or scientific proof of a hypothesis through experiment) and mathematical proof.

> There are, in principle, two basic ways of proof. If we are considering factual realities the proof consists mainly in producing or observing facts which will confirm the claim expressed in the respective statement. Our conviction of the validity of the statement will grow stronger as we become able to produce more facts which will fit the statement. With

reference to mathematics the way of proving is different: the statement we consider must be the logical, necessary conclusion of some other previously accepted statements. (p.15)

Intuitions relating to empirical proof are built up through practical activity. However, as Fischbein points out, "The concept of formal proof is completely outside the main stream of behaviour" (1982, p.17), and intuitions relating to formal mathematical proof are not developed in the course everyday activities. It is worth noting here that Fischbein believes that "a formal proof offers an absolute guarantee to a mathematical statement" (1982, p.17). Whether this is belief in a local guarantee within the formal system or a universal guarantee is unclear.

Even at the highest levels of formality, Fischbein (1982) argues that intuition plays an important role in proof:

> It is not enough for the pupil to learn formally what a complete, formal proof means in order to be ready to take complete advantage of that knowledge (in a mathematical reasoning activity). A new "basis of belief", a new intuitive approach, must be elaborated which will enable the pupil not only to understand a formal proof but also to believe (fully, sympathetically, intuitively) in the a priori universality of the theorem guaranteed by the respective proof. (p.17)

Here Fischbein is claiming that for the production of a formal proof to have any meaning for a student, they must have in place a suitable structure of intuitions and beliefs about the significance and properties of formal methods. However, these intuitions are of a different type to those concerning individual conjectures or propositions within mathematical systems; they are of a more general form providing convictions about the validity of the mathematical systems themselves. Without such intuitions students will not be capable of accepting a proof, and may still turn to empirical evidence for support of a conjecture (Finlow-Bates, 1994). Similarly, Kieran (1983) asserts that "a person's mathematical knowledge must be about experiences both externally referenced and internal and that formal mathematical knowledge must be based on informal knowledges for the person" (p.68).

In summary, from the above discussion on intuition and insight two main opinions as to the role of intuition within the area of proof can be extracted. The first, and most traditional, is that of intuition as a precursor to proof. Bruner (1979) presents the following summary of this belief:

> It is the intuitive mode that yields hypotheses quickly, that produces interesting combinations of ideas before their worth is known. It precedes proof; indeed, it is what the techniques of analysis and proof are designed to test and check. (p.102)

Here Bruner has reduced the role of proof to one of verification and justification, a role that was discussed in greater detail in an earlier section of this chapter.

However, there is a second, more recent view of intuition which sees its role woven into the whole of developmental process of mathematics, from the generation of conjectures, through to the most formal of proofs. Proponents of this view argue that at every stage in mathematics there are assumptions that are intuitively accepted, and that without these intuitive acceptances there would be no starting points and no progress. It is the immediacy of intuitive knowledge, along with the psychological barrier that needs to be overcome in order to question and examine in greater detail such knowledge that allows intuition to play such a role in mathematics.

Finally, I believe that the transition from intuitive to analytical knowledge is a two-way process, in that not only does intuition provide conjectures to be examined and tested through proof, but proof decomposes formal concepts into more readily understandable and intuitive ideas. This concept of proof as a decomposition is also discussed in greater detail from a Lakatosian perspective in chapter 5 on page 77. What is certain however, is that developing students' mathematical intuition plays an important role in developing their notions of proof.

3.7 Conclusion

Through an examination of the literature it has been shown that a variety of concepts such as generalisation, abstraction, communication, explanation, convincing, verification, intuition, and insight are all considered to play a part in developing an understanding of proof. However, there is no overall agreement on the precise meaning of any of these terms, nor is there general acceptance as to the exact relevance and importance of these aspects in developing broad and applicable notions of proof. I see no reason to add my own personal definitions or interpretations to the debate within this work. Rather, my aim has been through this chapter to review what has gone before and to flag areas I consider to be of interest or importance, although I have concluded each section of this chapter with a general summary of the aspects considered. The review of the literature continues in the next chapter when I consider a number of classification schemes put forward to categorise different types of proof.

4 Classification schemes for proof

4.1 Introduction

This chapter is concerned with examining what Balacheff (1988) has termed the "levels and types of proof" (p.216) that can be identified within the mathematics education literature. Proof schemas have been put forward in a number of published works most of which classify proofs according to their properties or level of formality in order to provide theoretical underpinnings for empirical studies aimed at interpreting students' behaviour when working with proof. Some of the proof schemas rely on particular theories of knowledge or learning, and where relevant, these theories are briefly reviewed along side the corresponding proof schema. It is difficult to identify a relevant sequence in which to present the identified proof classifications other than when one author's work relies on previous studies. As a result I have presented the sections of this chapter in what I personally perceive to be the most natural order.

4.2 Semadeni's action proofs

Semadeni (1984) introduces a form of generic proof called an action proof, the purpose of which is to provide "a general scheme for devising primary-school proofs" (p.32). Describing an action proof as "an idealized, simplified version of a recommended way in which children can convince themselves of the validity of a statement" (p.32), and thus identifying proof as that which convinces, Semadeni then presents the following description of what an action proof actually consists of:

> An action proof of a statement S should consist of the following steps:
>
> 1: Choose a special case of S. The case should be generic (that is without special features), not too complicated, and not too simple (trivial examples may later be particularly hard to generalize). Choose an enactive and/or iconic representation of

this case or a paradigmatic example (in the sense of Freudenthal [1980])

Perform certain concrete, physical actions (manipulation objects, drawing pictures, moving the body, etc.) so as to verify the statement in the given case.

2: Choose other examples, keeping the general schema permanent but varying the constants involved. In each case verify the statement, trying to use the same method as in 1.

3: When you no longer need physical actions, continue performing them mentally until you are convinced that you know how to do the same for many other examples.

4: Try to determine the class of cases for which this works. (p.32)

If by describing the generic as "having no special features" Semadeni means: "having no aspects that overshadow the properties we wish to abstract", then action proofs can be viewed as enactive/iconic generic proofs, within both Harel and Tall's, and Mason and Pimm's conceptions of the generic. Also, by claiming that "an action proof is a result of internalizing an action rather than a logical inference from given premises" (p.32), Semadeni is characterising this form of proof as a tool for engendering understanding and meaning in primary school children. It is worth noting here that Semadeni believes that "action proofs ... are valid mathematical proofs, that is, *provide absolute certainty*" (p.34, my italics).

Although there is no explicit reference to Bruner (1968), the use of the terms "enactive" and "iconic" place Semadeni's action proofs within Bruner's developmental theory. Mason (1980) provides the following interpretation of Bruner within this area:

ENACTIVE - able to respond only by recourse to previous practical experience.
...
ICONIC - able to respond by recourse to mental images of physical objects or to an inner sense of pattern or structure
...
SYMBOLIC - able to respond by using abstract symbols whose meaning must be articulated or defined.
(p.10)

Mason believes that the enactive in mathematics is not limited to primary school experience, but that even at a tertiary level and in the professional mathematics community mathematicians are working enactively. He suggests that "SYMBOLIC expression must ultimately become ENACTIVE if the idea is to be built upon or become a component in a more complex idea" (p.11), thus proposing that mathematical development, rather than being a simple progression from the enactive through the iconic and terminating at the symbolic level, consists of an enactive/iconic/symbolic spiral, with symbolic concepts acquiring meaning to then become enactive concepts of a higher level.

4.3 Walther's proof strategies

Walther (1984) expands Semadeni's action proofs to include action proofs which admit a transferral from the iconic to the symbolic, on the basis that the action proof schema can be applied, in certain situations to activities on the symbolic level:

> In my opinion it is not necessary to restrict the representation of action proofs to the enactive/iconic mode. Representation is only one aspect; it seems to be more important which kind of structured activity the enactive/iconic/symbolic represented (proof-) situation allows and demands. (p.10)

After discussing a model of proof involving dialogue between a "Proponent" and an "Opponent" (reminiscent of the latter part of Mason *et al.*'s (1982) "convince yourself, convince a friend, convince an enemy" problem-solving approach) in which the Proponent defends a conjecture from an Opponent's attacks, Walther (*ibid.*) states:

> From the psychological point of view it is obvious to try this defence with some special examples and to look for aspects of proof which are invariant regarding a transfer to other arbitrary examples. These invariants then constitute a proof-strategy for the general statement. (p.10)

From this we can see how Walther has tried to extend action proofs into the enactive/iconic/symbolic, rather than restricting them to the enactive/iconic as Semadeni does. Interpreting the above quote in the light of Mason's definitions of iconic and symbolic we can classify the discovery of "invariants" as iconic - namely the discovery or visualisation of a pattern, and then the construction of a "proof-strategy" as symbolic - namely the articulation of the invariant pattern discovered.

4.4 Balacheff's pragmatic and conceptual proofs

Balacheff (1988) defines two levels of proof, which he calls the pragmatic and the conceptual:

> ... pragmatic proofs are those having recourse to actual action or showings, and by contrast, conceptual proofs are those which do not involve action and rest on formulations of the properties in question and relations between them. (p.217)

Pragmatic proofs are essentially proofs on an enactive/iconic level, relying on "actions" (enactive) or "showings" (iconic) and as Balacheff admits, they have much in common with Semadeni's concept of action proofs. Conceptual proofs on the other hand are more symbolic in nature as they rely on "formulations of properties".

Within this framework of levels of proof, Balacheff identifies four approaches to proving, with each level constituting a transition to a more abstract notion of proof. Coe and Ruthven (1994) summarise these as follows:

> - nave empiricism in which the truth of a result is asserted after verifying several cases;
>
> - the crucial experiment in which a proposition is verified on a particular case recognised to be typical but non-trivial;
>
> - the generic example in which the reasons for the truth of an assertion are made explicit in a prototypical case; and
>
> - the thought experiment in which the operations and foundational relations of the proof are indicated in some other way than by the result of their use.
> (p.44)

The first three proof approaches are pragmatic, whereas the last is conceptual. Balacheff recognises that the first two proof approaches "do not establish the truth of an assertion; we talk of proof because they are recognised as such by their producers" (p.218). The boundary between a "crucial experiment" and a "generic example" therefore needs to be clarified. Balacheff suggests that "for the generic example and the thought experiment, it is no longer a matter of 'showing' the result is true because 'it works'; rather, it concerns establishing the necessary nature of its truth by giving reasons," (p.218) thus identifying reasoning as the fundamental difference between valid and invalid proofs.

4.5 *Blum and Kirsch's preformal proofs*

Blum and Kirsh (1991), in contrast to Balacheff, only identify three types of proof approach:

> Experimental "proofs"
> "Inhaltlich-anshaulich" or "intuitional" proofs
> Formal ("scientific") proofs
> (p.184)

Their "experimental proofs" are similar to Balacheff's "naïve empiricism", namely the verification of a finite number of cases. It is in their classification of intuitional proof as preformal proof (see Blum and Kirsh, 1991, p.189), and the inclusion of action proofs nand generic proofs as a form of (necessarily intuitive) preformal proof that Blum and Kirsh differ from both Balacheff and Semadeni:

> In accordance with Z. Semadeni's concept of "action proofs" (see Semadeni, 1984) we mean by a preformal proof a chain of correct, but not formally represented conclusions which refer to valid, non-formal premises. (p.187)

> An action proof (in a narrow sense) consists, in short, of certain concrete actions (actually carried out or only imagined) with a concretely given paradigmatic, generic example, where the actions correspond to correct mathematical arguments. (p.187-188)

For Blum and Kirsh the primary criteria as to what constitutes a preformal proof are that the argument on which it is based should be correctly constructed, and that its premises should be valid. This, they claim, is achieved by basing the premises and arguments on reality or intuition: "examples of such premises include concretely given real objects, geometric-intuitive facts, reality-oriented basic ideas, or intuitively evident, "commonly intelligible", "psychologically obvious" statements" (p.187). This claim raises a host of questions, such as: what constitutes a "real object", or a "basic idea", and how is a statement to be judged as "psychologically obvious" or "commonly intelligible".   In an attempt to side-step the philosophical can-of-worms they have opened, Blum and Kirsch write:

> What are "intuitive" or "obvious" bases for argumentation, has to be decided in each individual case by the persons involved on the basis of their knowledge. Such bases can, of course, be changed in course of time, in particular by learning or experience. (p.187)

Thus they present the assessment of correctness and validity as being personal, based on the individual's intuition and insight. Recognising that this leaves the question of what correctness and validity actually are open to the widest of interpretations they fall back on the argument "that it requires a competent mathematician to judge whether a given preformal proof is acceptable" (p.189). As a result Blum and Kirsh's argument, if indeed it can be construed as an argument, reduces to the belief that preformal proof relies heavily on mathematical intuition, and that the validity of these intuitions are ultimately to be judged by established mathematicians.

4.6 Van Hiele levels and proof

Although originally proposed as a model of learning geometry, the concept of van Hiele levels has been applied to proof, in particular to geometric proof. However most work concerning van Hiele levels still continues to be centred on geometrical understanding and reasoning (Burger and Shaughnessy, 1986, Lunkenbein, 1983). Bell *et al.* (1983) provide the following summary of the five van Hiele levels:

> Level I 'is characterised by the perception of geometric figures in their totality as entities ... judged according to their appearance. The pupils do not see the parts of the figure, nor ... relationships among components ... and among the figures themselves. The child can memorise the names of these figures relatively quickly, recognising the figures by their shapes alone.'

> In level II, the pupil 'begins to discern the components of the figures; he also establishes relationships among these ... and between individual figures. The properties of the figures are

established experimentally: the are described, but not yet formally defined.'

Pupils who have reached level III 'establish relations among the properties of a figure and among the figures themselves. The pupils are now able to discern the possibility of one property following from another, and the role of definition is clarified ... The order of logical conclusion is developed with the help of the textbook or the teacher.'

At level IV 'the significance of deduction as a means of constructing and developing all geometric theory' is recognised. The role of axioms becomes clear, and 'the students can now see the various possibilities for developing a theory proceeding from various premises.'

Level V 'corresponds to the modern (Hilbertian) standard of rigour. A person at this level develops a theory without making any concrete interpretation.'
(p.222-223)

Hoffer (1981) summaries these levels under the titles of recognition, analysis, ordering, deduction and rigour. Levels 4 and 5 are clearly closely related to the construction of proofs at a formal level whereas level 3, and to a certain extent level 2, can be seen as relating to proof at an informal level.

Van Hiele, quoted in Bell *et al.* (1983), illustrates the transition from one level to the next in the following statement:

At each level, the appears in an extrinsic manner what was intrinsic on the previous level. At the first level, the figures were in fact just determined by their properties, but one who is thinking at this level is not conscious of these properties.
(p.201)

Van Dormolen (1977) proposes a model of proof based on three levels, influenced by the van Hiele levels. At the first level, "the student is limited in his thinking to special objects" (p.32) and the students thinking is characterised as "specific". At this level the student is incapable of constructing any form of argument approximating a proof, and the student's conceptual organisation can be described as "local". This level of thinking is similar to the first van Hiele level.

At the second level the student forms links between objects, realising that "they all have something in common" (p.32). Arguments concerning a specific incidence are seen to relate to other examples, and elementary or informal proofs are constructed. This level of thinking is related to the second and third van Hiele levels.

At the third level the student "starts to realise that arguments on utterly dissimilar areas have elements in common. These arguments are in themselves examples leading to an understanding of what logical organization as such is. He can reason about reasoning" (p.32). At this point the student can critically evaluate the value of his or her own proofs and definitions and consciously restructure his or her mathematical systems. This level corresponds to the fourth and fifth van Hiele levels.

Van Dormolen summarises by writing:

> ... one could say that on a higher level of thinking one is able to effect an internal organization of the lower level. (p.32)

As van Dormolen himself freely admits, there is no simple solution to the problem of how students are to pass from one level to the next.

Senk (1989) has conducted an investigation into students ability to write geometry proofs based on the model of van Hiele levels. She found that: "The predictive validity of the van Hiele model was supported. However, the hypothesis that only students at Levels 4 or 5 can write proofs was not supported" (p.309). This supports van Dormolen's model of proof in which valid proofs are constructed at levels 2 and 3, corresponding to the van Hiele levels 2 through 5.

4.7 Lakatos' levels of proof

Lakatos' (1978) classification scheme relies on the level of formality of the proof in question and the position it holds within the development of mathematics. Lakatos recognises three primary categories: informal, quasi-formal and formal, depending on the format of the proof and the level of axiomatisation present within the deductive system in which it is situated. There is a sense in Lakatos' (1978, 1976) work that during the development of an area of mathematics its proofs become more formalised over time. Hanna (1990) provides the following description of a fully formal proof, with which Lakatos would probably have concurred:

> A formal proof of a given sentence is a finite sequence of sentences such that the first sentence is an axiom, each of the following sentences is either an axiom or has been derived from preceding sentences by applying rules of inference, and the last sentence is the one to be proved. (p.6)

Lakatos (1978) uses the well-defined notion of formal proof as a starting point to identify other levels of proof when he presents and discusses the following question:

> But what about an informal proof? Recently there have been some attempts by logicians to analyse features of proofs in informal theories. Thus a well known modern text-book of logic says that an 'informal proof' is a formal proof which suppresses mention of the logical rules of inference and logical axioms, and indicates only every use of the specific postulates.

> Now this so-called 'informal proof' is nothing other than a proof in an axiomatized mathematical theory which has already taken the shape of a hypothetico-deductive system, but which leaves its underlying logic unspecified. At the present stage of development in mathematical logic a competent logician can grasp in a very short time what the necessary underlying logic of a theory is, and can formalize any such proof without too much brain-racking. (p.62-63)

He suggests the term "quasi-formal proof" or "formal proof with gaps" to describe proofs that are in principle formalisable, whilst reserving the term "informal proof" to describe a proof situated in an informal theory.

Lakatos continues by identifying two types of proof - pre-formal and post-formal – in order to clarify the concept of informal proof. He defines a post-formal proof as an informal proof in an informal theory which has as its subject matter a formalised theory. Examples of this kind of proof include the consistency and completeness proofs of formal systems such as propositional calculus. To demonstrate the meaning of pre-formal Lakatos presents a brief informal proof of Euler's theorem (examined in more detail in Lakatos, 1976), and then makes the following comment:

> Now is this a proof? Can we give a definition of proof which would allow us to decide at least practically, in most cases, if our proof is really a proof or not? I am afraid the answer is 'no'. In a genuine low-level pre-formal theory proof cannot be defined; theorem cannot be defined. There is no method of verification.
>
> (Lakatos, 1978, p.65)

Lakatos states here that there is no practical definition as to what constitutes a pre-formal proof, other than that it takes place within an informal theory. That there is no formal definition for the informal should not be surprising. However, attempts have been made to provide informal definitions of pre-formal proof. For example, Hersh (1993, p.389) suggests that proof is: "convincing argument, as judged by qualified judges" . Although this definition has echoes of Russell's facetiously proposed definition of philosophy as "that which is studied in philosophy departments in our universities and colleges" (Hospers, 1973, p.55), it does provide a basis for discussion, and was considered in more detail in "Verification, justification, and convincing" on page 47.

Finally, the term "false" or "incorrect" proof can be used to describe a proof which, although taking the form of any of the proofs described above, would not be accepted by qualified judges as constituting a proof. There are many possible reasons for a proof not being accepted. Most depend on the theory in which the proof is presented. Thus a proof in a formal theory which uses a rule of inference not present in the axiomatic system would be incorrect. An informal proof might be rejected because it purports to prove a theorem for which there is an accepted refutation (for example, "squaring the circle" proofs), or because it generalises from a few limited, non-exhaustive cases. However, the issue of incorrect proofs is further complicated by the fact that an incorrect proof may occasionally cause a re-evaluation of the theory in which it takes place, resulting in the theory being changed, and the proof (possibly in a modified form) being accepted. This is one of the possible situations discussed in Lakatos (1976), which I examine in greater detail in chapter 5.

4.8 Summary and conclusions

In the above review a number of arguments aimed at organising proofs into different sets in accordance with their perceived properties have been examined. The aim of this process has often been to examine the ability of students to deal with proof, either explicitly (Balacheff, Semadeni, Coe and Ruthven, Walther, Blum and Kirsch, Senk) or implicitly (Hanna, Van Hiele, van Dormolen). In this section I summarise the proof schemas reviewed on the basis of the emphasis they provide on the aspects of generality and formality in classifying proofs. I conclude by rejecting the idea of developing a proof schema as a suitable method for investigating students' notions of proof in this study.

4.8.1 Summary

Semadeni (1984) and Walther (1984) both produced descriptions of a specific class of proofs which they called "action proofs", and which they believed to be highly accessible to students. In Semadeni's case the argument is that enactive/iconic action proofs can be used to induce primary school children to work with proof-like notions. Walther's work is an attempt to extend the action proof into the symbolic in order to draw in the formal aspect of proof. There are two points worth noting. Firstly, the prime characteristic used by Semadeni to identify a proof as an action proof is its generic-ness, thus the aspect of proof used to classify is the level and type of generality. Secondly, both Semadeni and Walther have used Bruner's (1968) enactive/iconic/symbolic developmental theory, with its obvious parallels to the levels of formality, in order to identify the place of action proofs within the overall scheme of proofs.

Balacheff (1988), on the other hand, presents a classification scheme for proofs based more on their level of formality present than their generality, by dividing types of proof into two categories: the pragmatic and the conceptual. His pragmatic proofs correspond roughly with Semadeni's and Walter's classification of the action proof as enactive/iconic. It is Balacheff's identification of conceptual proofs; proofs based on thought experiments; that provides his scheme with broader applicability. In the process of this identification Balacheff suggests the useful definition of a thought experiment as one in which the foundational relations and operations of the proof are indicated in some other way than by the result of their use.

Finally there are the schemes put forward by Blum and Kirsh (1991) and by Lakatos (1978), which use the level of formality present to classify proofs, and van Hiele's levels, which can be used to rank proofs according to their level of abstraction. Thus we see Blum and Kirsh talking about formal versus preformal proofs, and Lakatos about informal, semi-formal and formal proofs. Similarly van Hiele levels, as applied to proof by Senk (1989) and discussed by van Dormolen (1977), rely on levels of formality and abstraction, with corresponding levels of increased explicity in the methods used for the proofs.

4.8.2 Conclusion

The review of the literature presented in the last two chapters shows that a large number of proof schemas have been put forward in order to discuss proof and to classify students' abilities in dealing with it. Although a substantial quantity of interesting research has resulted from the idea that proofs can be neatly divided into different categories according to their properties (in particular on the basis of their level of formality, generality and abstraction), in my view adopting a similar approach now would be to participate in a process of stagnation. It has, after all, been two decades since Bell (1976) published his study of pupils' proof-explanations in mathematical situations, using a categorical approach based on the aspects of proofs and the levels and types of proofs evidenced. In the next chapter I develop a theory of proof based not on perceived levels or particular aspects of proofs, but on an overlooked central tenet drawn from Lakatos (1976) that proof consists of a thought experiment, suggesting a decomposition of a conjecture into lemmas and sub-conjectures. It is important to note that the theory constructed should be considered in the light of the literature discussed, with particular attention to Balacheff's (1988) outline of what constitutes a thought experiment in relation to conceptual proof and also the aspects of proof that were identified, as they provide an expansion of what it means to have a developed notion of proof.

5 Towards a theory on the nature of proof

5.1 Introduction

Kuhn (1962) has stated that "... something like a paradigm is prerequisite to perception itself" (p.113), and more recently Orton (1988) has claimed that "Meaningful inquiry is always guided by a theory" (p.36). A corollary of these observations is that meaningful inquiry will necessarily be interpreted in the light of a theory. This is as true of mathematics education as it is of any other subject. For this study the question then becomes: what theory should be used to guide and interpret an investigation into students' notions of proof?

Steiner (1987) has proposed that since "there is no distinguished, constant, universal philosophy of mathematics ... [one] should evaluate philosophies of mathematics according to their fruitfulness for particular goals and purposes and develop criteria for evaluation" (p.10). In this chapter I review the work of Lakatos on the nature of mathematical proof and the key role it plays in the development of mathematical knowledge. Then I consider a number of arguments which present mathematical knowledge as a kind of social knowledge. I argue that this conception does not reduce the value of mathematics, and is able to provide a richer perspective as to students' learning of mathematics, and of proof in particular.

The primary result drawn from this chapter is the use of the work of Lakatos (in particular his 1976) as a basic definition as to what constitutes a proof; namely that it consists of a thought-experiment, which suggests how an initial conjecture can be broken down into a set of sub-conjectures. The role of proof within mathematics is also examined, and it is concluded that not only does mathematics grow through "the incessant improvement of guesses by speculation and criticism, by the logic of proofs and refutations" (Lakatos, 1976, p.5), but that this process is inherently social in its nature, taking place in a culture and

77

language defined by both past historical traditions and current mathematical activities. The points raised in this chapter provide a theoretical framework for the investigation described in the second half of this book.

5.2 *Proof and the work of Lakatos*

For a full understanding of Lakatos' work it is necessary to comprehend what he means by his assertion that mathematics is "quasi-empirical" in nature (Lakatos, 1976, p.5). I believe this is best illustrated by the comparison of a quasi-empirical deductive system with its opposite — a Euclidean deductive system. In this context a deductive system consists of a set of premises or initial assumptions, a set of conjectures or final conclusions, and a collection of rules and definitions through which the conclusions are linked to the premises.

In a Euclidean theory we start with a set of initial statements or premises which are considered to be "trivially true or self-evident truths" (Dawson, 1969, p.70); these are usually labelled the axioms of the system. From the axioms using the given rules of derivation further statements can be derived. These derived statements are known as the theorems of the system. The whole system of axioms, rules of deduction and theorems constitutes a Euclidean deductive system. The Euclidean programme asserts that truth is transmitted from the axioms to the theorems by the rules of deduction. Thus if the initial axioms are true, truth flows downwards and pervades the system. Lakatos calls this the principle of transmission of truth (1986).

In a quasi-empirical deductive system, on the other hand, we start with a plausible conjecture. In attempting to explain the conjecture, assumptions or hypotheses are made, from which the conjecture can then be derived. This collection of assumptions, conjectures and rules of derivation constitutes the deductive system. In a quasi-empirical system the principle of retransmission of falsity (*ibid.*, 1986) applies. Simply put, this states that if the conjecture is shown to be false, then this refutation travels back from the conjecture to the hypotheses, falsifying them too. The whole structure then needs to be reconsidered. A second stricture is that it is never possible to know whether a conjecture is true because there is always the possibility that a new refutation will be found. This leads Lakatos to claim that "[a] Euclidean theory may be claimed to be true; a quasi-empirical theory - at best - to be well-corroborated" (*ibid.*, 1986). Quasi-empiricism is therefore a fallibilist epistemology of mathematics, with obvious parallels to Popper's Critical Fallibilist theory of science. Indeed, Lakatos acknowledges Popper in his (1976) with the statement that it "should be seen against the background ... of Popper's critical philosophy" (p.xii).

Lakatos' reason for contending that mathematics consists of quasi-empirical deductive systems, rather than any other type, is linked to the failure of other philosophical programmes to provide firm foundations for mathematics. Descriptions of the historical developments with regard to the search for foundations, and details of the various programmes put forward can be found elsewhere (see for example: Luchins and Luchins, 1965; Körner, 1962; Ernest, 1991). Broadly speaking the problem lies with the fact that any claim that mathematics demonstrates absolute certain truths fails due to the problem of infinite regress. That is to say a justification of such a claim requires a justification itself, and that justification requires a further justification, and so on ad infinitum. In the Euclidean programme this problem occurs at the level of the premises - we can never be sure that our "trivially true or self-evident truths" are actually trivial or self-evident, and history is full of examples where such premises have been shown to be false. Nevertheless Euclidean beliefs continue to be widely held by both teachers and mathematicians (Sconyers, 1995; Davis and Hersh, 1981).

Quasi-empiricism avoids the problem of infinite regress by claiming that we cannot know truth, or even if there is such a thing as truth. We can only guess and speculate, and through testing our guesses and speculations discard falsity, thereby developing mathematics. It is therefore a highly skeptical philosophy of mathematics. One way of looking at this philosophy is to regard mathematics as evolving away from falsity, as opposed to evolving towards truth. A second assertion is that mathematics grows through the invention of falsifiable conjectures, not through the discovery of indubitably true premises. The question now becomes: how does this growth occur? Lakatos proposes that once we have passed from the occurrence of a mathematical problem to the generation of a plausible conjecture, mathematics proceeds to advance through the logic of proofs and refutations.

5.2.1 *The logic of proofs and refutations*

Ernest (1994b) summaries Lakatos' logic of mathematical discovery as follows:

> ... a cyclic process in which a conjecture and an informal proof are put forward (in the context of a problem and an assumed informal theory). In reply, an informal refutation of the conjecture and/or proof are given. Given work, this leads to an improved conjecture and/or proof, with a possible change of the assumed problem and informal theory. (p.42)

Although this is a reasonable sketch of the method of proofs and refutations, it fails to communicate anything but the vaguest sense of what Lakatos actually meant. Part of the problem lies with the manner in which Lakatos' ideas are embedded in *Proofs and Refutations* (1976). It consists of an amusing, but obscuring "play" in which a variety of ideas are discussed by a classroom of Greek letters. In some cases Lakatos has his characters state opinions which he disagrees with, and although these opinions are usually later refuted, it is easy to quote them out of context. However, the greatest obstacle is that for Lakatos the word "proof" has a radically different meaning to its traditional use in describing an argument which proceeds along deductive lines.

Lakatos uses the word "proof" to mean "... a thought-experiment - or 'quasi-experiment' - which suggests a decomposition of the original conjecture into subconjectures or lemmas, thus embedding it in a possibly quite distant body of knowledge" (Lakatos, 1976, p.9). Thus a proof exists only in the minds of those who are engaged in proving, and need not take the form of an argument. When the lemmas and subconjectures are articulated, or written down in an ordered list, what is produced is a proof-analysis (*ibid.*, p.12). The advantage of this view of proof is that "... the decomposition deploys the conjecture on a wider front, so that our criticism has more targets" (p.10). It is therefore consistent with a fallibilist philosophy of mathematics.

One requirement of a proof is that it should be possible to conduct the thought-experiment that it outlines, albeit in ones head. Thus Lakatos has Kappa criticise the teacher for causing a proof to disappear, when one of the lemmas in its proof-analysis is shown to be false and is replaced with an unfalsified lemma which is ambiguous. In this situation the proof-analysis therefore no longer suggests a clearly executable thought experiment, or proof (*ibid.*, p.12). It is worth noting here that the relationship between proof and proof-analysis work both ways, that is to say: the proof suggests the proof-analysis, and similarly the proof-analysis points towards the proof.

One of the advantages of Lakatos' definitions of proof and proof-analysis is that they allow counterexamples to be classified (Dawson, 1969, p.115). When a counterexample is discovered, it will either refute the conjecture, the proof, or both. In each case, Lakatos identifies the possibilities open to mathematicians for dealing with the refutation. These are discussed below.

5.2.1.1   *Local counterexamples*

Lakatos calls a counterexample to the proof but not the conjecture a "local counterexample" (Lakatos, 1976, p.10). Local counterexamples suggest that there is a flaw in the proof, and typically refute one of the lemmas of the proof-analysis. The conjecture remains unfalsified. There are a number of ways to proceed:

1. The option of surrender. The proof and conjecture are discarded and a new problem is investigated.

2. Incorporate the falsified lemma into the conjecture (*ibid.*, p.57). This strategy restricts the domain of the conjecture to that of the proof, thereby excluding the counterexample. The disadvantage is that the scope of the conjecture is drastically narrowed, and many interesting and valid cases of the original conjecture may be forgotten. In some cases this strategy may actually reduce our mathematical knowledge.

3. Replace the falsified lemma with an unfalsified one (*ibid.*, p.58). This involves improvement within the framework of the original proof and according to Lakatos it is the usual procedure adopted by mathematicians when initially discovering a local counterexample. Deeper understanding of the conjecture within this framework is then obtained. It is an *ad hoc* method, because there will never be a guarantee that the new lemma will not at some point be falsified. Usually the counterexample suggests an unfalsified replacement for the "guilty lemma", but in some cases it may be too difficult to find such a replacement. In

this case there remains one more option:

4. Search for a new, deeper proof (*ibid.*, p.59). This option raises an interesting question: will the new proof prove the same conjecture as the old proof? Lakatos contends that "Different proofs yield different theorems" (*ibid.*, p.65), or in more evolutionary terms: " ... one ... conjecture is improved by each proof into a different theorem." (p.65). I believe this to be too strong a contention, because although the new proof will in all likelihood include examples dismissed by, and fail to include examples proved by the old proof, there should be a large overlap between the two. Bloor (1983) presents the same problem, as posed by Wittgenstein:

> The proof of a mathematical proposition, claims Wittgenstein, enriches and therefore changes its sense. How, then, can there be two different proofs of the same proposition? Each proof would endow it with a special sense, so there will be two different propositions where before there was only one. (p.103)

Although Wittgenstein is talking about mathematics in a social manner, he reaches similar conclusions along pragmatic lines, as is shown by Bloor (1983) when he continues:

> Wittgenstein dismisses this objection. It depends, he says, on 'what we choose to say settles its sense'. If both proofs demonstrate that the proposition is a 'suitable instrument for some purpose', then we can say they prove the same proposition. (p.103)

5.2.1.2   *Global-and-local counterexamples*

A counterexample to the conjecture but not the proof is called a "global counterexample" by Lakatos (1976, p.11). Because an understanding of how to deal with counterexamples to both the proof and the conjecture (*i.e.* global-and-local counterexamples) is necessary to understand purely global counterexamples, I shall review them first. A global-and-local counterexample refutes the conjecture, and one or more of the lemmas in the proof. Lakatos identifies five approaches for dealing with them, which Dawson (1969, p.114) erroneously attributes to global-but-not-local counterexamples:

1. The method of surrender (Lakatos, 1976, p.13). The

counterexample is accepted as valid, and the conjecture is rejected. The problem is returned to for the production of a new conjecture, or in extreme cases even the problem is discarded. Lakatos criticises this method for its defeatism.

2. The method of monster-barring. (*ibid.*, p.14). Terms used in the conjecture are clarified or redefined to specifically exclude the counterexample. As Dawson (1969) points out, this method rejects "... the counterexample as not REALLY being a counterexample which, of course, allows one to retain the original conjecture" (p.116). The thought-experiment, or proof, remains unchanged, as does our conception of the conjecture. Lakatos claims that: "Using this method one can eliminate any counterexample to the original conjecture by a sometimes deft but always *ad hoc* redefinition ... " (1976, p.23). Furthermore, monster-barring does not provide more insights, and it certainly does not create more mathematics. It simply entrenches and preserves the original conjecture. The two main criticisms of this method are the arbitrary manner in which counterexamples are overcome, and the stifling effect it has on the growth of mathematical knowledge.

3. The method of exception-barring (*ibid.*, p.24). Lakatos presents Beta as a proponent of this method, who claims: "I accept the method of monster-barring in so far as it serves for finding the domain of validity of the original conjecture; I reject it in so far as it functions as a linguistic trick for rescuing 'nice' theorems by restrictive concepts." (*ibid.*, p.26). Exception barring is an enlightened form of monster-barring. It functions by rechristening counterexamples as "exceptions" (*ibid.*, p.25), which are examined to discover why they are not covered by the initial conjecture. In the light of this examination the conjecture is then restricted to exclude the exceptions, and the proof is restricted to ensure it contains no false lemmas. The main problem is that in restricting the conjecture to exclude the exceptions, some examples that satisfied the initial conjecture may also be excepted - that is to say, the initial conjecture may be restricted too severely. A secondary problem is that, like the method of monster-barring, it is *ad hoc* in its treatment of counterexamples (*ibid.*, p.30).

4. The method of monster-adjustment (*ibid.*, p.30). In the case of monster-adjustment the counterexample is re-interpreted, to indicate that what was first seen as a global counterexample is in fact a legitimate example in favour of the initial conjecture. The conjecture therefore remains unaltered. As Lakatos has Rho say: "... where you - erroneously - 'see' a counterexample, I teach you how to recognise - correctly - an example." (*ibid.*, p.31). Dawson (1969) points out that "this is a dogmatic response to counterexamples; the theory of perverted vision is employed to explain why some individuals cannot see what is manifestly true." (p.119). Monster-adjustment can be described as a form of monster-barring applied to the counterexample rather that the conjecture, and the same criticisms apply.

5. The method of lemma-incorporation. (Lakatos, 1976, p.33). This manner of dealing with global-and-local counterexamples typifies what Lakatos means by "the development of mathematics through the logic of proofs and refutations". The proof is examined to determine which lemma has been refuted by the counterexample. This "guilty lemma" (*ibid.*, p.34) is then added as a condition to the conjecture, which is then no longer refuted by the counterexample. Lemma-incorporation differs from all the above methods in that it utilises properties of the proof, the conjecture and the counterexample to overcome the refutation. This leads Lakatos (*ibid.*) to claim, through the medium of the teacher, that:

> [P]roofs, even though they may not prove, certainly do help to improve our conjecture. The exception-barrers improved it too, but improving was independent of proving. Our method improves by proving. This intrinsic unity between the 'logic of discovery' and the 'logic of justification' is the most important aspect of the method of lemma-incorporation. (p.37)

A second advantage of lemma-incorporation over exception barring is that it does not overly restrict the domain of the conjecture. As Lakatos (*ibid.*) says:

> ... while the exception-barring method restricted both the domain of the main conjecture and of the guilty lemma to a common domain of safety, thereby accepting the

84

counterexample as criticism both of the main conjecture and of the proof, my method of lemma-incorporation upholds the proof but reduces the domain of the main conjecture to the very domain of the guilty lemma. (p.34).

The final advantage of lemma-incorporation is that it is not *ad hoc* , as it provides a prescribed method of dealing with all global-and-local counterexamples. To conclude, the method of lemma-incorporation involves proof-driven improvement of the conjecture by adding the refuted lemmas as conditions to the conjecture to overcome the counter-example. Lemma-incorporation is the most suitable approach to a global-and-local counterexample from a fallibilist perspective, as it relies on the fact that if the counter-example refutes the conjecture then it must refute a part of the proof.

5.2.1.3   *Global counterexamples*

Finally, the third type of counterexamples consist of those which are global only, *i.e.* they refute the conjecture but not the proof. From a fallibilist viewpoint truly global-but-not-local counter-examples cannot exist - the principle of retransmission of falsity demands that a counterexample which falsifies the conjecture must falsify one of the lemmas into which the conjecture can be decomposed. The methods of surrender, monster-barring and monster-adjustment as described above can be used to deal with a global-but-not-local counterexample, although the deficiencies ascribed to them still apply. Lakatos identifies two more approaches:

1. The method of hidden lemmas (*ibid.*, p.43). On closer inspection of the proof it is discovered that the global-but-not-local counterexample is actually a global-and-local counterexample, refuting a "hidden lemma" which was implicitly assumed to be part of the proof. The hidden lemma, which was previously seen as an obvious truth, is then re-interpreted as an obvious restriction on the conjecture. Proponents of the hidden lemma method claim that "[a] hidden lemma is not an error: it is a shrewd shorthand pointing to our background knowledge" (*ibid.*, p.45). The method of "smuggling a reserve of 'hidden lemmas' into the proof and corresponding 'hidden conditions' into the theorem" (*ibid.*, p.47) is labelled as

dogmatic by Lakatos. He notes that although supporters of the hidden lemma method may think that careful inspection of the proof will "yield a perfect proof-analysis containing all the false lemmas" (*ibid.*, p.47), and that through lemma-incorporation the conjecture may become a "perfected theorem" (*ibid.*, p.47), there is never any guarantee that no more global-but-not-local counter-examples will arise.

2. The method of proofs and refutations (*ibid.*, p.47). The conjecture is discarded, and a lemma which is refuted by the counterexample is added to the proof-analysis. The discarded conjecture is then replaced by a new conjecture incorporating the refuted lemma, as in the lemma-incorporation method above. This ensures that the counterexample will not refute the improved proof or the new conjecture. In this process all "hidden lemmas" are made explicit as soon as they are discovered (*ibid.*, p.48), which opens them up for criticism. Lakatos considers the method of proofs and refutations to lie at the heart of the development of mathematics.

This concludes the review of the role played by refutations in the development of proofs, and the classification of types of counterexamples and methods for overcoming them. It is now appropriate to continue with a discussion on the origins of initial conjectures and their proofs.

5.2.2 *The origins of conjectures and proofs*

Dawson (1969) notes that "The proving phase of mathematical inquiry follows after some mathematical conjecture has been corroborated" (p.112). He labels this stage in which the mathematical conjecture is obtained the "origination phase" (*ibid.*, p.129). This phase is important for two reasons - firstly the shape which the initial conjecture takes will greatly affect the form taken by its proof, and secondly in some cases the origination phase can result in the production of a proof as well as a conjecture. It is generally recognised that there is no definitive answer as to how conjectures are obtained but "[w]hat is possible, however, is to provide some suggestive patterns, patterns which may have a wide range of applicability even if they do not have universal applicability and success." (*ibid.*, p. 89). Lakatos (1976) identifies two heuristics in which conjectures are obtained. The first is naïve guessing in which the conjecture precedes the proof and which is related to the work of Polya (1957, 1967). The second is deductive guessing, in which the conjecture is obtained through the construction of a proof. Both processes start with an examination of a problem.

5.2.2.1 naïve guessing

In the process of naïve guessing the conjecture is obtained through observation; that is, through the examination of data. The data is obtained through the investigation of specific examples that arise from the problem. Many conjectures may be put forward only to be refuted and discarded before one arrives at a conjecture sufficiently plausible to merit proving.

In schools in Britain the procedure of producing a conjecture frequently consists of examining a large number of examples, drawing up a table, and inferring a general rule (Hewitt, 1992). This is a form of naïve guessing. The general rule inferred is often called an inductive conjecture. Lakatos (1976), however, argues that there is no such thing as induction, and that:

> naïve conjectures are not inductive conjectures: we arrive at them by trial and error, through conjectures and refutations. (p.73)

If induction is taken to mean the recognition of a pattern somehow external to the conjecturer then I agree with Lakatos when he states "there are no such things as inductive conjectures" (*ibid.*, p.73). However, if the term induction is merely used to describe the process of conjecturing through trial and error by using a sizeable quantity of data selected and ordered in some personal fashion, then I believe it is indeed possible to conjecture inductively. Induction is then to be viewed as a psychological process, related to our tendency to form generalisations and construct patterns. An in-depth examination of this process is regrettably beyond the scope of this study.

Polya (1986) firmly believes in inductive reasoning, which he identifies as consisting of generalisation, specialisation and analogy. Generalisation in this context consists of postulating that a property known to apply to a limited number of cases may also apply to a much larger number of similar cases, as was discussed in more detail in chapter 4. It is worth noting that conjectures often take the form of generalisations. Specialisation can be seen as a reverse process of generalisation, in which a general rule is tested on a limited number of cases. Dawson (1969) writes:

> [I]n attempting to solve a problem, it may be fruitful to look at a special case of the problem, to limit its scope, and to make the conjecture relative to the specialization rather than the whole problem at once. In this way some clues as to the solution of the more general problem may be obtained. (p.93)

The final method of conjecturing identified by Polya is reasoning by analogy. Polya (1986) defines an analogy as follows:

> Analogy is a sort of similarity. It is, we could say, similarity on a more definite and more conceptual level. ... The essential difference between analogy and other kinds of similarity lies, it seems to me, in the intentions of the thinker. Similar objects agree with each other in some aspect. If you intend to reduce the aspect in which they agree to definite concepts, you regard those similar objects as analogous. (p.104)

Thus a known conjecture from one problem may originate a new conjecture in an analogous problem. naïve guessing, as its name suggests, is the more basic heuristic for conjecture origination. Lakatos (1976, p.73) recognises that indoctrination into the naïve guessing procedure may cause one to forget the alternative: deductive guessing.

5.2.2.2   *Deductive guessing*

Contrary to naïve guessing, deductive guessing starts with an idea (Lakatos, 1976, p.70) obtained by a close examination of the problem. The idea leads, through a deductive sequence of conclusions, to a conjecture. The conjecture therefore comes with its own proof-analysis, in the form of the sequence of conclusions that spawned it. In elucidating where the initial idea originates, Lakatos has Zeta state:

> Instead of collecting data I trace how the problem grew out of our background knowledge; or, which was the expectation whose refutation presented the problem? (p.70)

For example, Zeta claims the initial idea leading to the Euler conjecture, namely that V-E+F=2 for polyhedra (where V is the number of vertices, E is the number of edges, and F is the number of faces), arises deductively from the knowledge that for a polygon in three dimensional space V-E+F=1 and is driven by the fact that the equation for the polygon does not hold for most polyhedra (*ibid.*, 1976, p.71). It is arguable whether the initial idea is obtained through naïve guessing or through a deductive process; however, what matters is that the conjecture which it results in is obtained deductively.

Deductive guessing has an inherent advantage over naïve guessing, in that it always produces an initial proof. A common problem when attempting to engage students in proving, is that although they are capable of producing generalisations through naïve guessing, they often lack the impetus to then proceed to a proof (Reid, 1995b). Hewitt (1992) suggests that one reason for this could be that generalisation from a set of numerical examples can cause them to forget the original problem. However, Lakatos (1976.) notes that although "[D]eductive guessing is best, ... naïve guessing is better than no guessing at all" (p.73).

5.3 *Proof as a kind of social knowledge*

Once we accept the idea that proof consists of a thought-experiment suggesting a decomposition of the conjecture into sub-conjectures, a questions arises: what provides the thought-experiment and proof-analysis with their convictive power; what is the deeper nature of these two concepts? In the following sections I address this question by examining social perspectives on some of the generalities concerning the nature of mathematical proof and the practices surrounding it. Specific functions and aspects attributed to proof are considered in more detail in the light of this discussion in chapter 3, "Aspects of proof". The adoption of a quasi-empirical theory of proof based on a social theory of knowledge is by no means imperative, as is discussed at the end of this section. I will show, however, that it provides us with useful ways in which to view proof, and with which to consider students' activities when they are engaged in proving. In this discussion although I will be drawing on the work of many differing social accounts of mathematics I do not intend to align myself with any specific one. For the purposes of this discussion, and the classroom investigation it documents in its second half, such an alignment is not strictly necessary. A full defence of a particular social theory of knowledge is also far beyond the scope of this work, as is the construction and execution of an empirical investigation designed to elucidate the social nature of mathematical knowledge. The usefulness of a social approach to mathematics has however already been evidenced above with, for example, Wittgenstein's assessment of the role of different proofs of the same conjecture. Furthermore, given the qualitative nature of the investigation documented in chapter 7, a deeper discussion of the researcher 's beliefs concerning the nature of mathematical knowledge, underlying the Lakatosian theory developed in the first half of this chapter, can only help place in context the observations made and the conclusions drawn in the investigation.

Ernest (1994b, p.34) identifies, amongst others, accounts of mathematics as a "culture", a "social system", a "language", and as "conversation". A synthesis of these different accounts is in all probability impossible, but they all hold in common the idea that mathematics is a product of human invention, as opposed to consisting of external discovery of eternal facts. In this sense, social theories of knowledge are in many ways dialectically opposed to a Platonistic epistemology, and often were conceived to overcome the deficiencies therein. Bloor (1983) summarises the Platonistic view as follows:

> Platonism is the view that mathematical results are discoveries about a special realm of objects that exist prior to our knowledge of them. Arithmetical propositions are true because they correspond to facts about entities called 'numbers'. Geometry informs us of the relations between idealised entities called 'points' and 'lines'. Advocates of this view have never fully explained the mode of being, of, say, numbers, or clearly described how they intermingle with ordinary material objects. All they do is stress that they are different, more basic, and never change. (p.84)

The Platonistic view is considered to be the commonly held default philosophy of most mathematicians - Rotman (1988) calls it the "orthodox position representing the view of all but a small minority of mathematicians" (p.5), and Davis and Hersh (1981) have expressed similar sentiments. It carries with it the belief that there must be absolute criteria for the truth of mathematical statements, and is as such in opposition to quasi-empiricism. Some mathematics educationists appear to suggest that a fallibilist epistemology of mathematics, such as quasi-empiricism, automatically carries with it a social theory as to the nature of mathematical knowledge (*e.g.*, Ernest, 1994a). I am not convinced this is necessarily so. Lakatos refuses to commit himself to a theory as to the ontological nature of mathematical knowledge in *Proofs and Refutations*, much as Popper does in his critical fallibilism, preferring instead to discuss how mathematicians develop mathematics. It is therefore possible to construct theories of the nature of mathematical knowledge with no social element which can be coupled with quasi-empiricism. For example, a severely weakened version of Platonism in which it is argued that mathematical entities have an existence beyond our knowledge of them, but with a clear concept of such entities and a knowledge of their truth being eternally elusive to the mathematician, would satisfy this. However, quasi-empiricism's fallibilistic nature does place it diametrically opposite the stronger Platonistic philosophies which claim that the properties of mathematical entities are essentially self-evident, and that the truth of propositions concerning these entities can be firmly established. This opposition with Platonism suggests to me that quasi-empiricism should instead be regarded as being well suited to a social interpretation.

In the following overview I have tried to discuss social theories of mathematics in a reasonably ordered fashion. Mathematics and proof are examined as originating from a historical and cultural structure (Restivo, 1992, 1993; Kline, 1980), as a "conversational" or "dialogical" phenomenon (Ernest 1994b, 1991; Bloor, 1983, 1994) and as part of a language system (Pimm, 1987; Rotman, 1987, 1988), although there is an overlap between all these categorisations.

5.3.1 *Cultural and social accounts of proof*

What are the differences between theories regarding mathematics as cultural and social forms of knowledge? Lerman (1994), in trying to illustrate the difference between "cultural" and "social", writes as follows:

> ... I find myself slipping form the word 'culture' to 'social'. These terms are not interchangeable but nor are they simply separated. One would perhaps think of gender stereotypes as cultural, but of 'gender' as socially constructed. One would talk of the culture of the community of mathematicians, treating it

as monolithic for a moment, but one would also talk, for example, of the social outcomes of being a member of that cultural group. (p. 2)

I would argue that a possible and useful distinction between the two is that "the social" is primarily synchronic in nature, whereas "the cultural" is diachronic. Therefore, although we may well have a passing interest in the cultural origins of our knowledge and practices in mathematics, we label such knowledge as social due to our focus on mathematics as it is currently perceived in our community. Along similar lines, Restivo (1993) draws the distinction between social developments in the past, and current thinking when he states:

> The social aspects of mathematics, then, have two dimensions: historical (in the embodiment of past operations now reduced to thing-like representations, tools and machines) and contemporary (each mathematician is implicitly and explicitly negotiating with - cooperatively or conflictually - his/her community over what problems are worthy of attention, what methods are appropriate, and what solutions will be acceptable). (p.266-267)

There have been a number of studies relating various mathematical concepts, as they stand today, to their historical origins and development. For example, Hanna (1983) and Kline (1980) both draw upon the history of mathematics to support their theses about the relevance of rigour in mathematics education, and the loss of mathematical certainty respectively. Restivo (1992) argues that mathematical views have been inexorably shaped by the courses taken by cultures through history. He gives as an example the ancient Chinese forms of mathematics, which were developed along rhetorical lines with only a limited concept of proof by our Western standards (Siu, 1993). This, Restivo claims, is due to the lack of a cohesive mathematical community, which itself is a product of the political situation of the time. The rulers of Ancient China saw the formation of an academic community as a threat to their power structure, thus relegating the pursuit of scholarship to a solitary affair.

Like Lakatos and Polya, Restivo contends that mathematics starts with the formulation of a problem. However, for Restivo, the origins of these problems are cultural. For example he argues that problems concerning commerce can give rise to new forms of arithmetic, and problems concerning land ownership or architecture can result in the construction of a theory of geometry. As a culture develops these theories can gain respect in themselves, as opposed to being regarded simply as tools. In this sense, mathematics then becomes a kind of sport. For the ancient Greeks, for example, problems such as squaring the circle or trisecting the angle "became the basis of a mathematical game of challenge-and-response" (Restivo, 1992, p.11). The rules under which this game was to be conducted, although significant to the culture in which they were developed, can be considered as arbitrary as the culture itself. Similar observations have been made about the role of mathematics in renaissance Italy (Restivo, 1992). Restivo (*ibid.*) asserts that not only do the problems on which we focus change during the development of society, but the basic beliefs we hold concerning apparently central notions such as truth, reasoning and number are also altered. He provides the following examples:

> In the course of the nineteenth-century development of algebra, the concept of mathematical truth changed from "objective" (based on a relationship to reality) to "abstract" (based on formal criteria of completeness and consistency). This change reflected changes in the social structure of the mathematical community...
> (p. 103)

> Consider the proof that no fraction p/q could ever precisely equal the square root of 2. Does the proof prove that the square root of two is not a number (Aristotle), or that it is an irrational number (modern mathematics)?
> (p. 109)

In the light of this exposition it becomes increasingly difficult to assert that a society can develop methods of deriving and describing absolute truth. Proof becomes yet another societal quirk.

5.3.2 Proof and language

In this century we have seen the emergence and development of social theories of knowledge including mathematical knowledge, relying on concepts such as language, dialogue, conversation, or "talk". For example, Restivo (1993) presents the following "insights":

> ... all talk is social; the person is a social structure; and the intellect (mind, consciousness, cognitive apparatus) is a social structure. These insights are the foundation of a radical sociology of mathematics. (p.248)

Elsewhere he connects the "technical talk" of mathematics to humanity's general "social talk", to argue that mathematics is therefore also a social phenomenon.

> Whereas "technical talk" isolates mathematics from other social practices (thereby "spiritualizing" the technical), social talk links mathematics to other social practices, *and reveals the social nature of technical talk itself.* (Restivo, 1992, p.ix, my italics)

Whether we speak of the "talk", dialogue, conversation, or language of mathematics, one aspect remains constant; ultimately the mathematical developments are to be communicated between members of the mathematical community, and to belong to this community it is necessary to communicate in accordance with the accepted modes and within the bounds of the traditions that it has adopted. It is from the collectiveness of the community that we obtain a sense that the mathematics we develop is in some sense true and external to us. Bloor (1983) writes:

> ... the compelling force of mathematical procedures does not derive from their being transcendent, but from their being accepted and used by a group of people. The procedures are not accepted because they are correct, or correspond to an ideal; they are deemed correct because they are accepted. (p.92)

Restivo (1993) presents similar sentiments when he writes:

> The apparently purest concepts, logical concepts, take on the appearance of objective and impersonal concepts only to the extent that and by virtue of the fact that they are communicable and communicated - that is, only insofar as they are collective representations. (p.249)

Ernest (1994b) claims that conversation can be understood on three levels: intrapersonal, interpersonal and cultural. The most obvious level of conversation is the interpersonal one. It constitutes "one of the basic modes of interpersonal human interaction, perhaps the most basic one" (p.36), and includes speech and "all forms of notation, diagram, and materially embodied complexes of signs" (*ibid.*). Moving up one level we can then define cultural conversation as "the direct sum of interpersonal conversations" (*ibid.*). Finally, and most controversially, there is the definition of intrapersonal conversation as a form of internalised interpersonal and cultural conversations. This idea can be found in the works of amongst others Vygotsky, Bakhtin, and, possibly in a broader sense, Wittgenstein. Interpersonal and cultural levels of conversation have been addressed in the above discussion. Although I find the concept of intrapersonal conversation as an internalisation of the two higher levels to be one of great interest, a full examination thereof is not necessary here nor is it within the scope of the study.

5.3.3 A semiological account of proof

Although not strictly scientific in Popperian terms, semiotics has been defined as "the science of signs" (Berger, 1982, p.14). It is concerned with how meaning is generated in "texts", which can be seen to include mathematical texts, writings and discourses. Semiotics provides a descriptive language to talk about and analyse such texts, and has been used to examine the role of proof in mathematics. For example Ernest (1995) has presented a tentative semiotic account of proof, in which he argues that writings in mathematics signify "an imaginary, textually defined realm" in which proof involves "carrying out imagined text based actions" in a well-defined cyclic manner.

The central tenet of semiotics is that meaning is generated and conveyed through relationships between signs. A sign can be divided into two components, the signifier which is an actual "physical" entity (a sound or image) and which represents the signified concept. A second tenet of semiotics is that the relationship between the signifier and signified is arbitrary (Berger, 1982). These distinctions have a potentially useful application in our Lakatosian definition of proof. The proof, or thought experiment, can for example be seen as the signified, suggesting a decomposition of the conjecture or proof-analysis which can be seen as the signifier. These semiotic definitions can provide an effective way to consider the relationship between proof-as-thought-experiment and proof-analysis.

A further semiotic assertion is the existence of codes. Berger (1982) defines codes as "highly complex patterns of associations we all learn in a given society and culture" (p.30). Mathematics, contrary to most sign systems, contains numerous codes that can be relatively easily articulated in an explicit manner, such as the rules of formal logic or the law of the excluded middle. However, many more codes remain implicit, and thus we can speak about mathematical enculturation, or induction into the world of mathematics, as a learning of the codes that apply therein.

The semiotic concepts of signs, signifiers, signifieds and codes can be used to provide a semiotic description of systems. For example Rotman (1987) provides the following abstract model which can easily be applied to both formal and informal systems of mathematics:

> There is a system ... which provides a means of producing infinitely many signs ... . These signs re-present items in what is taken to be a prior reality ... for an active human subject ... . The system allows the subject to enact a thought-experiment ... about this reality through the agency of a meta-sign ... which initiates the system and affects a change of codes ... . (p.27)

The system could be anything from a formal axiomatic system to an informal mathematical system relying on the English language (or any other language) for an expression of its statements. These statements are then the signs of the system. What is "taken as a prior reality" need not be a Platonic reality. The signified of a sign of the system may be a signifier for something else, and so on in an increasing chain of signs, with the original concept becoming lost in translation. As Rotman (1987) elucidates:

> ... a simple picture of an independent reality of objects providing a preexisting field of referents for signs conceived after them, in a naming, pointing, ostending, or referring relation to them, cannot be sustained. What gives this picture credence is a highly convincing illusion. Once the system is accepted, on the basis of a perfectly plausible original fiction, as a mechanism for representing some actually, it will continue to claim this role however far removed its signs are from this putative reality ... (p.27-28)

Although this indicates why mathematics need not be platonic in nature, it still fails to explain why through logical argument and proof we can become convinced of the truth of a proposition. Rotman (1988) addresses this, the final touchstone of any social approach to mathematical knowledge, in a manner similar to that of Restivo and Bloor in the previous section, albeit from a semiological perspective:

> Mathematicians believe because they are persuaded to believe;
> so that what is salient about mathematical assertions is not
> their supposed truth about some world that precedes them, but
> the inconceivability of persuasively creating a world in which
> they are denied. Thus, instead of a picture of logic as a form of
> truth-preserving inference, a semiotics of mathematics would
> see it as an inconceivability-preserving mode of persuasion –
> with no mention of "truth" anywhere. (p.34)

When we exchange proofs with other mathematicians we can see
this as entering into an arena bound by codes and conventions,
with implicitly defined and understood chains of signifieds and
signifiers. Some of these codes and conventions were examined in
greater detail in chapter 3, "Aspects of proof" and chapter 4,
"Classification schemes for proof".

5.4 An illustrative example

In the previous sections of this chapter a theory of the nature of
proof was developed, introducing a number of theoretically defined
concepts such as naïve and deductive conjecture, thought
experiment, and proof-analysis. In this section I provide concrete
examples with which to come to grips with these elements of the
theory.

The examples I use are based on a modified version of a
conjecture and proof put forward by Sconyers (1995), concerning
the dissection of a polygon. It should be noted that Sconyers
describes proof in his article with phrases such as "necessary
inference", "the conclusion must be accepted", and as something
that is "logically unassailable", which are phrases at odds with my
characterisation of proof and also, as this section will show, with
the occurrences in his classroom and surrounding the publication
of his paper. A closer look at the practices surrounding the
development and refinement of the proof provides a useful means
for the illustration of the theory and concepts developed in this
chapter, and simultaneously the theory sheds light on some of the
aspects of the activities in Sconyers' classroom hitherto
overlooked.

A final introductory note is required: the analyses and
observations drawn in this section are in some cases made on the

basis of "straw polls", and are not meant to be regarded as conclusions obtained from methodologically grounded empirical experiments. Rather, they should be seen as illustrations of the various concepts and procedures outlined in this chapter.

5.4.1 The origination phase

It was claimed in this chapter that the proof process starts with the examination of a problem. In the case of Sconyers' proof the problem arose in the following manner:

> While working on polygons with a group of students, a problem led us to model convex octagons on a geoboard and using Logo. It became useful to draw a line segment to divide a convex polygon into two new polygons. Among several interesting questions generated was this one:
>
> Begin with a convex polygon with a given number of sides. Connect two points with a segment. How many sides do the two resulting polygons have altogether?
> (Sconyers, 1995, p.517)

In the example given by Sconyers the students continued by constructing a table and empirically examining the increase in the number of sides. This is a clear example of naïve conjecturing. The conjecture resulting from this process was that the new polygons have a total of two, three, or four more sides than the original polygon.

I have presented the Sconyers problem to a number of friends and colleagues since I discovered it. In all but one case a conjecture was arrived at through naïve conjecturing. The exception was in the case of a friend who had studied mathematics at degree level. He deduced a similar version of the conjecture listed above by constructing a rough proof-analysis through the analysis of a number of different polygon dissections as in the next section. This was the only example of deductive conjecturing I encountered in my straw polls.

5.4.2 A proof-analysis and thought experiment

Once the students in Sconyers' class settled on a conjecture, the following argument was put forward:

1. The segment goes from vertex to vertex. Two more sides result than the original. Why? Each original side is a side in one of the new polygons. Also, the segment itself is a side of each new polygon. The group has a net increase of two sides.

2. The segment cuts two sides. Four more sides result than the original. Why? Each of the two cut sides becomes two sides in the new polygons, for a net gain of two sides. Also, the segment itself is a side in each new polygon. The total net gain is four sides.

3. The segment goes through a vertex and cuts a side. Three more sides result than in the original. Why? The cut side becomes two sides, for a gain of one. The segment itself adds two new sides. The total net gain is three sides.

No other possibilities exist. (Sconyers, 1995, p.518)

This argument illustrates the concepts of proof-analysis and thought experiment. The argument written out above is a proof-analysis, in that it breaks down the original conjecture into three sub-conjectures. The decomposition relies on a thought experiment indicating how the original conjecture is to be broken down. How this thought experiment is visualised differs from person to person. I have heard descriptions such as "I see the three cases drawn on paper", or "I see a paper polygon being cut repeatedly in different ways using scissors or a guillotine". I would imagine that some of Sconyers' students would see a thought experiment in terms of the geoboard they were working on, or in terms of a Logo robot, given that these are the tools they were working with during the formulation and examination of the conjecture. However, the principle remains the same, in that a generic polygon is dissected in the mind's eye in ways indicated by the proof-analysis. Furthermore, the proof-analysis provides a level of conviction by pointing towards a thought experiment which appears to cover all the possibilities.

5.4.3 A brief examination of some social issues

Before looking at the next phase in the cycle of proving and refuting, there are a number of social issues worth examining. These issues are also significant in the context of the next section on refutation and how it developed the notions of some of the people to whom I presented the Sconyers conjecture.

The first issue concerns the concept of a polygon. There is no indication in Sconyers' work that "polygon" was explicitly defined in the course of the students' work, and similarly in my straw polls I presented participants with a minimal amount of information to deal with the problem. But despite not having a clear concept of what constituted a polygon (in the context of the problem), the participants were capable of working on the conjecture, and developing their knowledge of polygons, often into new and sometimes unorthodox areas.

Another issue following on from this, which arises from the conjecture as presented by Sconyers in his article, involved further investigation. I was initially surprised to find the word "convex" in a problem to be considered by American middle school pupils. Similarly a spot-check on 15 people working in mathematics education at the University of Wisconsin-Madison suggested that when asked to draw polygons people initially draw convex ones by default. Communication with the editor of Mathematics Teaching in the Middle School revealed that the first draft of the paper presented to the journal did not in fact contain the word "convex" in the conjecture. It was only after proof-reading revealed a counter-example that the paper was changed to include the convexity condition. However, this change is not readily obvious in the final presentation, providing a clear example of how mathematics can be "sanitised" to conceal the procedure of proofs and refutations, and in particular to hide that proof does not provide a guarantee of absolute certainty.

A final social issue worth noting is the ubiquitous presence of the participants in my descriptions of examples of the elements in the theory of proof. The examples given do not stand well on their own; the environment in which they were constructed, the history, and to a certain extent the personalities behind their development all play a role in illustrating the principles of the theory.

5.4.4 Counterexamples and possible resolutions

Sconyers concludes the proof-analysis in his article with the statement that "no other possibilities exist" (1995, p.518). Further examination of the problem has shown this not to be the case, and a number of counterexamples and further possibilities for refinement are discussed.

In the section above an account of the inclusion of the word "convex" was discussed. This inclusion was due to the discovery of a global-and-local counterexample to the proof, namely that there existed polygons which were cut into three shapes by a segment from a point on the polygon's perimeter to another point on the perimeter. An example is given in figure 5.1:

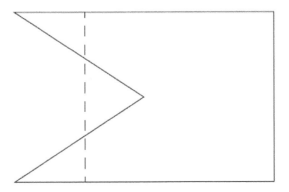

Figure 5.1 A counter-example to the original conjecture

Sconyers used the method of exception-barring to overcome the counterexample, by restricting the domain of validity of the conjecture to include only convex polygons. However, this excludes some perfectly valid examples, as many of the cuts made through the polygon in figure 5.1 do not refute the conjecture at all. Secondly, the counterexample is overcome by only considering the conjecture, and not the proof-analysis, thus improving independently of proving. Finally, the method used is *ad hoc*, in that it provides little insight into how to overcome any future counterexamples.

A different proposal made to overcome the non-convex polygon counterexample was to only allow line segments entirely contained in the polygon for the purpose of dividing the polygon, as shown in figure 5.2:

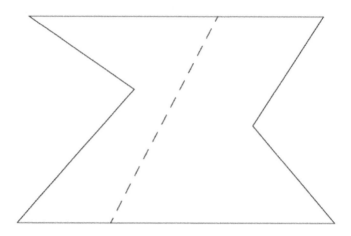

Figure 5.2 Restricting the use of line-segments

This method, the method of proof and refutation, has advantages over the exception-barring method for several reasons. Firstly, the basis on which the refutation of the old conjecture rests is revealed by examining the proof-analysis and uncovering that the second lemma has been falsified by the counterexample. The new conjecture is then obtained by recasting the old one to read "the number of sides of a polygon divided using an internal cut increase by 2, 3, or 4." thus improving the conjecture by using the proof. The domain of the conjecture is not overly narrowed, and a greater understanding of the counterexample is gained.

Further counterexamples were put forward in some of my straw polls. I shall present one of the most significant. It is a counterexample to the conjecture as it stands in Sconyers (1995) paper. It consists of the four-sided polygon depicted in figure 5.3:

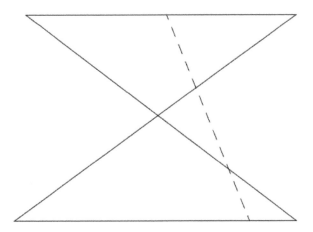

Figure 5.3 Another counter-example

This polygon was put forward as a convex shape which refuted the conjecture because some cuts across the polygon, such as the one illustrated, divide it into three new polygons with an increase in sides of eight. The counterexample refutes both the conjecture and lemma 2 of the proof-analysis, making it a global-and-local counterexample. I have come across a number of approaches to overcome this counterexample. Two of the clearest examples are listed here:

1. The method of monster-adjustment. One monster-adjusting solution was to reinterpret the shape in figure 5.3 as two triangles joined at one vertex; thus the shape has five vertices and six sides, rather than four vertices and four sides. It is no longer a simple convex polygon and the conjecture and proof remains unaltered. This case is analogous to the case of the stellated dodecahedron in *Proofs and Refutations* (Lakatos, 1976, p.31). Another monster-adjusting solution was to re-interpret the shape as not being convex, by taking two of the angles to be less than 180° and the other two angles to be greater than 180°, as in figure 5.4:

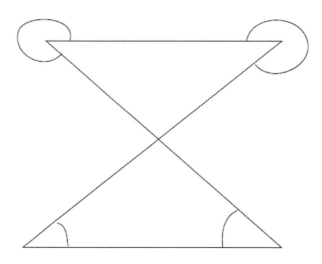

Figure 5.4 A monster-adjustment

2. The method of monster-barring. A suggestion put forward by one participant was to bar all polygons in which the vertices cross. This is a classic example of monster-barring, as no insight is gained into why the shape in figure 5.3 was a counterexample, the proof-analysis was not used in re-casting the conjecture, and the domain of the new conjecture is reduced to such an extent that many examples that fitted the old conjecture are no longer considered.

To conclude, in this section a problem has been examined to illustrate the various elements of the theory of proof developed in this chapter. It has illustrated the approach of taking proof to be the coupling of a proof-analysis and thought experiment, and proving as the cyclic process of conjecturing, constructing a proof-analysis, exposing the proof-analysis to criticism through the emergence of counterexamples, and recasting the conjecture and proof-analysis to overcome the refutation. Finally, it informally suggests that a Lakatosian approach to proof presents a richer and more authentic view of the process of proving than the dogmatic view of proof as absolute final evidence of truth. In the next section of this chapter, a summary of the theory is presented and conclusions are drawn.

5.5 Conclusions and summary

Lakatos presents proof as a thought experiment consisting of the decomposition of the conjecture into sub-conjectures and lemmas. Proof suggests a proof-analysis; proof-analysis being an articulation of the decomposition. Echoes of these definitions can be found in the thoughts of the mathematician Stanlislaw Ulam (1976) when he writes of his own experiences of proof:

> Clearly only the one-dimensional chain of syllogisms which constitutes thinking can be communicated verbally or written down. Poincaré (and later Polya) tried to analyze the thought process. When I remember a mathematical proof, it seems to me that I remember only salient points, markers, as it were, of pleasure or difficulty. (p.180)

The "one-dimensional chain of syllogisms" is in this sense an ordered proof-analysis, suggested by a previous thought experiment. It is not surprising that this list is not remembered in detail - it is reconstructed. Instead the "salient points" are what is kept in mind, and these form the core ideas of the proof's thought-experiment. The proof-analysis serves two purposes: firstly it is a means to communicate the proof to others; a prompt to assist them in reconstructing the thought-experiment of the proof, and secondly it provides a wider target for the process of development through refutation and the discovery of counterexamples.

For the purposes of this study I am adopting Lakatos' view as the central definition of proof. The roles commonly attributed to proof, such as justification, explanation, logical argument, articulation of a generalisation, and suchlike will be viewed as characteristics of some proofs; roles that, although important and so frequently enacted as to appear to embody the nature of proof, are ultimately secondary to the central definition.

The role of the counterexample in the development of proofs and conjectures has been examined. Three types of counterexample have been identified, as well as the possible ways in which to deal with them. These possibilities are summed up in table 5.1 below:

Table 5.1 *Methods for dealing with counterexamples*

Local only	Global only	Global-and-local
Surrender	Surrender	Surrender
Lemma-incorporation	Monster barring	Monster barring
Lemma-replacement	Monster-adjustment	Exception-barring
Find a deeper proof	Hidden lemmas	Monster-adjustment
	Proofs and refutations	Lemma-incorporation

It has been argued that from a fallibilist perspective the ideal manner of overcoming a counterexample is through the method of proofs and refutations, which relies on the process of lemma-incorporation and making all hidden assumptions explicit.

The manner in which initial conjectures are obtained, and their relation to the construction of proofs has been investigated. Two approaches were identified: naïve guessing and deductive guessing. In naïve guessing the conjecture is proposed through a process of trial and error, and once a sufficiently interesting and corroborated conjecture is suggested and tested a proof is embarked on. Deductive guessing is proof-driven conjecturing - the conjecture is obtained through reasoning from a set of initial assumptions and comes complete with its own proof. Successive refinement of the conjecture in both cases then occurs through the discovery of further counterexamples, as outlined above. The methods of deductive and naïve guessing are illustrated in figure 5.5 below:

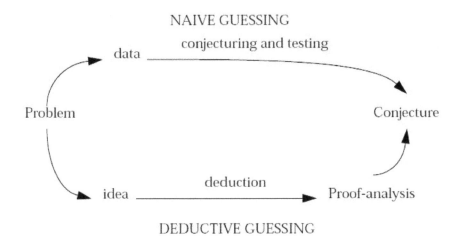

NAIVE GUESSING

Figure 5.5 Heuristics for obtaining an initial conjecture

It is important to be aware that the above diagram is not a strict description of how conjectures are obtained; for example the deduction of a conjecture from an idea may involve some testing of the basic steps of the deduction, ideas may be obtained from data and vice versa, and so on. What is important is that the diagram provides a summarised overview of the two guessing strategies identified.

I have also briefly reviewed a number of social perspectives on the nature of mathematical knowledge from the cultural level through the level of mathematics as a language or dialogue down to the level of the customs and codes exhibited within a community. It can be argued that some of the social aspects of mathematics in general and proof in particular are concealed by the widely held convention within the mathematics community that mathematics is "real", and that there exist means to discover absolute truths, particularly through the medium of proof. Furthermore a number of arguments were presented to indicate how a social theory of the nature of mathematical proof can account for the strong sense of predetermination and conviction that proof carries; aspects of proof often used to support arguments asserting the Platonistic nature of proof and mathematics. Finally, a vocabulary has been introduced with which social phenomena of proof can be talked about in a meaningful manner.

In conclusion, in the classroom when we speak about a student possessing developed notions of proof, what is meant is whether or not the student can work with proof in a recognisable manner. What might constitute such a "recognisable manner" is usually left unsaid. In this chapter I have identified the central concept of a proof as a thought experiment, with a corresponding proof-analysis which can be seen as a pointer towards the proof.

5.6 Recent criticisms of Lakatos' work

A number of criticisms have recently been levelled at Lakatos' work by Hanna (1996). Although her criticisms have little bearing on the main structure of the current study, it seems relevant to consider them in the context of my discussion of Lakatos above. Hanna manifests her concerns in three different areas: the accuracy of Lakatos' characterisation of the growth of mathematical knowledge through proofs and refutations, the rejection of Euclideanism in favour of fallibilism in quasi-empiricism, and the dismissal of formal mathematics by educators on the grounds of Lakatos' work.

Hanna expresses concern at the supposed failure of the method of proofs and refutations to explain some important examples of mathematical discovery. Examples that are presented include set-theory research, the acceptance of the Zermelo-Fraenkel axioms, the emergence of non-standard analysis, and "many mathematical discoveries that did not start with a primitive conjecture" (p.28). It is not clear to me how the above are to be considered as refutations of Lakatos' views on mathematical discovery. In particular I find it hard to visualise "the acceptance of the Zermelo-Fraenkel axioms" as a discovery. Furthermore, Hanna appears to have overlooked that Lakatos' heuristics for obtaining conjectures can provide an explanation for some of the other cases listed. Indeed through deductive guessing, in which a conjecture which need not necessarily be "primitive" is arrived at by tracing how a problem grows out of background knowledge (Lakatos, 1976, p.70), mathematical discoveries can be made without starting with a conjecture.

Secondly, Hanna rejects the coupling of fallibilism with the method of proofs and refutations, arguing that mathematicians undertake this heuristic "for the purpose of arriving at certainty" (p.29). She claims that "in the case of Euclid's theorem, for example, the long heuristic process did lead, in fact, to a proof which satisfies the accepted criteria of mathematical certainty." (p.29), and quotes Hacking (1979) in claiming that Euler's theorem has been proved to be true. In Hanna (1995) we are confronted with an even bolder general statement: "A proof that proves shows that a theorem is true" (p.48). I am not clear on what the "accepted criteria" are for mathematical certainty and truth, but even if such criteria were presented to me I would find it hard to forget that history is littered with examples of mathematical "truths" that were later refuted and standards of working that were later rejected.

Finally, Lakatos was not trying to reject formal mathematics *per se* in *Proofs and Refutations*. Rather, he was rejecting: that the formalisation of mathematics was the ideal way to resolve at least partially the crisis in the foundations of mathematics, that formal structures in mathematics were a way of obtaining indubitably true theorems, and that the increasing axiomatisation of mathematics was to be striven for at the expense of all else. However, with regard to those educators who wish to excise formal mathematics from the curriculum, I would side with Hanna. Formal mathematics has an important role to play in the classroom, and to discard it is to deny our mathematics students access to a valuable part of our mathematical heritage.

6 Methodology and design of the investigation

6.1 Introduction

The main investigation consisted of the audio-taping, transcription and analysis of the conversations of a group of four first year mathematics students as they worked on a set of question sheets. The taping took place in November 1994, during two 4 hour sessions of the Mathematical Contexts and Strategies course at South Bank University in London. South Bank University does not offer a mathematics degree, although some of its degree courses, such as the BSc Mathematics and Computing for Decision Making and the BSc Joint Honours in Mathematics and Computing have a strong mathematical bias. One of the aims of the Mathematical Contexts and Strategies course is to present topics to such students from a mathematical perspective, and it is therefore taught as though the students were studying mathematics for its own sake. The course was team-taught by myself and one other member of staff.

In order to provide a clear considered methodology for the main investigation I discuss a number of historical, practical and theoretical issues underlying its design and execution in this chapter. The discussion culminates in the adoption of a qualitative research methodology accounting for the nature of the investigation in relation to its theoretical basis and the environment in which it takes place, as well as the traditions and practices of the field in which the research is conducted. Then I present the full method and design of the study, in order to clearly describe how and under what conditions the investigation was carried out, and what procedures were followed in the process of transcribing of the tapes, the analysis of the transcriptions, and the writing up of the report presented in chapter 7. Finally I consider issues surrounding the reliability and validity of the study and present a summary of the chapter.

6.2 *Background*

An overview of mathematics education literature concerned with examining how students deal with proof, such as the one I presented in chapters 3 and 4, clearly reveals the value placed on conducting empirical research to develop and/or examine theory. The role of the empirical research with regard to theory varies, as do the research methods; for example Moore (1994) has used non-interactive observation followed by interviews to develop grounded theory *a posteriori* (Glaser and Strauss, 1967), whereas Balacheff (1988) has conducted interactive experiments and observations to "support the *a priori* analysis made of the [proof] procedures and conceptions that the pupils would bring into play" (p.221) during problem solving sessions. Common research methods currently include the interview (for example: Coe and Ruthven, 1994; Chazan, 1993), the questionnaire (Finlow-Bates *et al.*, 1993; Schoenfeld, 1989) and both interactive and non-interactive observation (Reid, 1995b; Moore, 1994; Balacheff, 1988; Schoenfeld, 1988).

The preliminary research leading up to the major investigation detailed in this work (see chapter 2, "A review of the preliminary research") showed an increasing trend towards the use of more qualitative methods during the development of theory and methodology, and the conducting of the pilot empirical work. Initially in Finlow-Bates *et al.* (1993) I used a questionnaire to investigate what concepts of proof were held by first year mathematics students. At that point in the research I had not yet dealt with the intricate details and complexities surrounding the question of what actually constitutes proof. The questionnaire contained an essentially quantitative section designed to determine which arguments, purporting to prove a theorem about triangle, were considered to be proofs by the students. The questionnaire also contained some open-ended questions about the arguments presented and about the students' experiences with proof in their previous schooling.

One of the unexpected results of the initial study was the indication that the open-ended questions revealed more about the students' notions of proof than the quantitative data. This led to a second study (Finlow-Bates, 1994) conducted on the following year's intake for the same course. In this study I used an adapted form of the discourse-based interview introduced by Odell and

Goswami (1982) and adapted to an academic setting by Herrington (1985). The study showed both an increasingly developed research method and methodology, and a clearer theoretical background, which was reflected in the insights that were provided and the conclusions that were drawn.

The major study described in this chapter and the next, represents the main section of the empirical research that started with the research reported in Finlow-Bates *et al.* (1993).

6.3 *Theoretical considerations*

In the previous four chapters I discussed a number of philosophical, epistemological and educational issues concerning the nature of mathematical proof, culminating in the development of a Lakatosian and social theory of proof. The aim of this was two-fold; firstly I wished to provide a new perspective on proof, and secondly I required a clear theoretical framework to underpin an investigation into first year mathematics students' notions of proof. In this section issues concerning the designing, conducting and interpretation of this investigation in the light of the theory are considered.

A conclusion drawn from the theoretical basis for proof was that proof cannot be examined in isolation, but that the community in which it takes place must also be considered. This is as true of our current community of university mathematics researchers as it is of any of the mathematical cultures that existed in the past. Treatises that were considered proofs by those cultures are sometimes no longer regarded as such, and similarly what is considered to be a proof by the standards of today may, and in all probability will, be rejected in the future, to the extent that some writers have even predicted the imminent demise of proof (Horgan, 1993). Although recognising that globally proof is in flux, studies in the past of students' notions of proof implicitly take the approach that on the local level of the investigation there are correct proofs towards which the students should be working, and their success in dealing with proof is measured by how near they get to these ideal proofs.

As a result, in this study I take the fresh approach that although a group of students may not produce a rigorous, polished proof, they may exhibit behaviour suggesting that they are heading in such a direction, or are developing their own standards and protocols fulfilling a similar role. Assessing students' notions of proof merely by examining whether or not they can produce a finished proof ultimately fails to take into account any understanding they may have exhibited during the process of working.

A final issue that arises concerns the relationship between the theory of proof based on Lakatos' work, and the environment to which it is applied, namely the classroom. Initially there would appear to be a question as to the validity of the analogy between the context of learners working to solve problems and mathematicians seeking to prove theorems. However, this question of validity can be answered on two fronts. Firstly, although the students working in the classroom were often engaged in problem solving, the structure of the worksheets presenting the problems was open. This resulted in the students having to, in effect, set their own problem solving agendas and investigations, and thus proving and problem solving were interlaced. Secondly, Lakatos describes the origination phase of mathematical development commencing with a problem, from which the context for proving arises. Thus, according to Lakatos, mathematicians are also involved in both problem solving and proving in their work. As a result there are more parallels between the working of students and of mathematicians than appeared initially.

6.4 Scope and focus of the investigation

In this section the theory of proof is split into three parts, and the relation of each part to the investigation is considered. In particular, the omission of an explicit examination of the social dimension of the theory in the investigation is justified.

6.4.1 The definition of proof and proof-analysis

The "top" level of the theory is directly concerned with the nature of mathematical proof, and defines it as thought experiment coupled with proof-analysis. Investigating how students engage in developing notions of proof in the light of this definition forms a key focus of the investigation, and the second half of the investigation presented in chapter 7 deals specifically with this part of the theory. In particular, the events surrounding the development of two proofs, indicated by the construction of a proof-analysis (presented on page 148) and the description of a thought experiment (see page 164) are examined in detail.

6.4.2 Quasi-empiricism and fallibilism

At the "middle" level of the theory is Lakatos' quasi-empirical account of the nature of mathematics, which forms an important foundation to the definition of proof detailed above. It is important from a theoretical point of view, in that the notion of a proof-analysis is presented by Lakatos as a means of providing a greater number of targets for the falsification process in mathematics. It is also highly significant from the point of view of the investigation, in that the students must develop conjectures in order to begin to engage with proving. The question sheets on which the students work in the investigation provide scope for the formulation of conjectures on the limits of sequences initially, followed by opportunities to prove those conjectures. An examination of the whole process, from conjecture to proof is therefore necessary, in order to avoid isolating the proof process from its origins.

6.4.3 The social nature of mathematical knowledge

Lakatos' description of mathematics as quasi-empirical, developing through the process of proofs and refutations, provides an account of the logic of mathematical discovery. However, as was discussed in chapter 5, no explicit ontology is presented in Lakatos' account. In order to strengthen my theoretical basis for proof and to present it more clearly in the context of my own beliefs, I discussed the concept of mathematical knowledge as social knowledge in the second half of chapter 5, concentrating in particular on how such a designation does not preclude the capacity of such knowledge providing us with strong convictions. In a sense, this part forms the "lowest" or most basic level of the theory. From a pragmatic point of view, adopting a social basis for mathematical knowledge has already proved useful in, for example, resolving the problem of different proofs proving the same theorem (see page 82).

The question remains, to what level is this social view of mathematical knowledge to be examined in an empirical investigation of the theory. It is obvious that, on an inter-personal level, there is a clear social element present in any classroom, and this is acknowledged in the report in chapter 7. For example, the relationship between the teacher and the students influences the direction taken when working on mathematical problems (see W's intervention on page 136), as do interactions between the students themselves (Phi blatantly ignoring a counterexample on page 133 is a clear example of this).

From a more fundamental point of view the analysis of mathematics as a social form of knowledge through a research study presents a number of problems. I can envisage a local study of the social nature of mathematical knowledge, such as a continuation of the Sconyers' (1995) problem, in which a new (for the teacher as well as the students) open-ended question is set, with the inventions of the class as the mathematical constructions of the moment. Such a study is not conducted in this investigation for the following reasons:

1. Placing the investigation in such a setting would not constitute an examination of the students in a natural setting (the relevance of this with regard to qualitative research is discussed later in this chapter, on page 118).

2. More significantly, widening the scope of the study to attempt to empirically elucidate the social nature of mathematical knowledge would detract from the focal point of the study, which is to examine students' notions of proof.

Finally, a more global study, in the sense of inventing new mathematics for the professional mathematical community is harder to envisage, and would in any case suffer from problem 2 outlined above, as well as presenting severe practical difficulties. Therefore a "weak" social view is an essential focus of this study, in the sense of Brodie (1994), with the social interactions of the students perceived as a key element in the formation and investigation of conjectures, and hence in the development of proofs. The "strong" social view must remain part of a potential future programme of research.

6.5 Methodological issues

A methodology can be loosely defined as the system of principles, practices and procedures applied to a specific branch of knowledge. A clearly stated methodology allows others to make informed assessments about the relevance and usefulness of the research by considering what assumptions have been made by the researcher, how the research proceeded, and how the results obtained inform the theory underlying it. The lack of a clearly outlined methodology can unfortunately reduce a detailed analysis of a transcript to the level of mere anecdote.

It is recognised that in any form of qualitative research there will be a certain level of subjectivity due to the pre-perceptions and prejudices of the researcher. A well designed methodology can draw attention to these and allow them to be minimised. Concepts within qualitative research which are therefore of particular concern are the internal consistency of the work and the clarity, explicity and reasoned justification of the arguments and methods adopted.

Finally, there are fundamental differences between research projects studying school classroom interactions, and those examining university level classes. Age disparities apart, the primary difference is that university students are assumed to have chosen to continue their education, whereas school children are required to be in their classroom by law. This is evidenced in for example the minimal role a university lecturer plays in maintaining class discipline, and the length of time a group of university students can work on question sheets unsupervised. These differences cannot avoid having an influence on the study, although they are not readily quantifiable.

6.6 *A qualitative research methodology*

Echoing the sentiments of Kuhn (1962) and Orton (1988) quoted at the start of chapter 5, albeit from a methodological perspective rather than a theoretical one, Fetterman (1989) notes that:

> Theory is a guide to practice; no study, ethnographic or otherwise, can be conducted without an underlying theory or model. Whether it is an explicit anthropological theory or an implicit personal model about how things work, the researcher's theoretical approach helps define the problem and how to tackle it. (p.15)

An example of this within the field of mathematics education is the constructivist teaching experiment as devised by Steffe *et al.* (1983), which Steffe describes as being "derived from Piaget's clinical interview" (p.177) and which is carefully designed to suit constructivist epistemology. Steffe notes that:

> A distinguishing characteristic of the technique is that the researcher acts as teacher. Being a participant in interactive communication with a child is necessary because there is no intention to investigate teaching a predetermined or accepted way of operating. (p.177)

Teacher conducted research has since become a well established tradition within mathematics education (Owens, 1993; Wilson, 1993), thus validating my dual role as both a lecturer for the Mathematical Contexts and Strategies course and as a researcher collecting data from the classroom and interpreting it, in the process of conducting the investigation. Furthermore, during the process of lecturing the course my interactions as a researcher were limited to the setting up and operating of the recording equipment, and interpretation only took place after all the data had been gathered.

Marshall and Rossman (1995) note that "design exibility is a crucial feature of qualitative inquiry" (p.14). It is simply not possible to outline categories to account for all possible occurrences and their moderation within all possible contexts that can arise within the classroom, as was also noted at the end of chapter 4, "Classification schemes for proof" with the dismissal of a proof classification scheme as a basis for the study. The nature of the investigation is therefore exploratory rather than experimental:

> In exploratory studies, a scientist has no clear idea of what will happen, and aims to find out. He has a feeling for the direction in which to go ... but no clear expectations of what to expect. He is not confirming or refuting hypotheses. (Harr and Secord, 1972, p.34)

Bogdan and Biklen (1992, p.29-32) identify five key characteristics of qualitative research. I will briefly discuss the relation of each to my study from a theoretical and a practical view in turn:

1. Qualitative research has the natural setting as the direct source of data and the researcher is the key instrument (p.29).

A conclusion arising from the theoretical framework, discussed in the section above on theoretical considerations, was that the process of developing notions of proof needed to be examined in a holistic manner. Thus rather than repeating the investigative methods of the preliminary research which consisted of students filling in a questionnaire or being interviewed in isolation, I decided to observe how students dealt with notions of proof in a group situation by conducting the main study in the natural environment of the classroom. This is one of the aspects of the research that clearly reveals the relevance of a qualitative methodology to the theory.

A direct consequence of placing the study in the classroom is that as the arbitrator and primary interpreter of the events occurring in the classroom in relation to the research, the researcher is placed in the role of "key instrument" for the study. This is the case in my investigation, which is carried out in an environment in which I was the course designer and lecturer for the duration of the class, with a cassette deck recording the students' activities, and subsequently acted as an informed researcher when interpreting the results. A further effect of this is that, as a researcher who was present in the classroom and who knew the participants, there is an extra level in my interpretations, albeit subjective, which relies on more than the words contained in the transcriptions. I account for this in the analysis of the transcriptions by explicitly indicating where interpretations made relied strongly on personal knowledge and interpretation.

2. Qualitative research is descriptive (p.30).

A distinguishing feature of most qualitative research is the absence of large numbers of tables containing numerical data. This is not surprising as qualitative research, as its name suggests, does not involve the interpretation of events in a quantitative manner. The specific details of my transcript analysis and the report are presented in the next section, although it is clear from the next chapter which contains the report write-up that my research is descriptive. Events in my study are interpreted during the analysis of the transcripts, and are not processed and collated using a specified formulaic or statistical method.

3. Qualitative researchers are concerned with process rather than with outcome (p.31).

Teaching and learning are inherently concerned with outcomes, in that they are goal-directed processes aimed at developing knowledge in the learners (Brodie, 1994), or even from a cynical point of view, in that they are aimed at gaining the learners qualifications for improved prospects. However, when focusing on learning outcomes with regards to students' notions of proof it is all too easy for the researcher to conclude that the students encounter nothing but difficulties. For example, Moore's (1994) study contains seven categories to classify student failings in understanding formal proof, but none to account for success. By concentrating primarily on proof as a process, as discussed at the end of chapter 2, "A review of the preliminary research", I illustrate in chapter 7 how students can succeed in developing notions of proof, even if these notions do not provide them with the ability to construct or evaluate rigorous proofs. To illustrate, in the report of the analysis one of the students succeeds in constructing a proof-analysis pointing to a thought experiment which, although fundamentally flawed and therefore not a "correct" proof, still indicates an understanding of proof according to my interpretation, which would not be evident under a more outcome-based analysis.

On a more basic level, my analysis in chapter 7 is concerned with process in that it analyses the students' conversations and work holistically as they make progress through the worksheets. It draws out links between the achievements of their early and their later work, and shows how they build upon their developing skills. For example, my analyses of the students' work in constructing a proof makes explicit reference to their earlier activities in producing a conjecture to prove – indeed, the analysis would be significantly weakened without such reference.

4. Qualitative researchers tend to analyse their data inductively (p.31).

Of the five points made by Bogden and Biklen it is this one I believe to be least relevant to the investigation. The intended interpretation sees inductive data analysis as a means of generating theory from data, as in for example the development of grounded theory presented by Glaser and Strauss (1967), suggesting that qualitative research tends be *a posteriori*. As was discussed in Section 6.2 on page 112, this was not the aim of my work. Furthermore, as the theory has already been applied to a report by Sconyers (1995) of a classroom situation in "An illustrative example" on page 97 with good results, this potential phase of the research has passed. Instead, an aim of the investigation was to continue the application of the theory to actual classroom events; which in the instance of the investigation in chapter 7 are first-hand to the researcher, rather than second-hand as was the case in the analysis of Sconyers' classroom.

The difficulty with this point can therefore be overcome by noting that the nature of the investigation is exploratory rather than experimental, and that my aim is not to empirically verify an explicitly stated hypothesis. Instead it is my intention to present an informed and supported theory – one that has been utilised or "tempered", as it were. Cobb, Yackel and Wood (1992) note the cyclical nature of such investigations when they state that "particular events empirically ground theoretical constructs, and theoretical constructs inform the interpretation of particular events." (p.100). It is in the light of this statement that the relationship between the study and the theoretical framework can be examined. Initially I had conceptions of what might constitute proof as suggested by a review of the literature. Without such initial theoretical underpinnings the empirical study could not have been conducted. However, the theory as it is presented in this work has been subject to moderation in the light of the study in a dynamic process of feedback and feed-forward, with the empirical evidence suggesting the level of appropriateness and relevance of some of my theoretical notions of the role and nature of proof. As such this work is at best a selection of snapshots of a continuous process.

5. "Meaning" is of essential concern to the qualitative approach (p.32).

To analyse students' notions of proof is to grapple with how students try to understand. Concepts such as "understanding", "learning" and "meaning-making" are not readily quantifiable. We can however provide tentative descriptions of what we mean by "an understanding of", interpret students' behaviour in the light of such descriptions, and through such activity come to a more informed understanding of what it means to understand.

From the perspective of the investigation presented in chapter 7, "meaning" and "understanding" are paramount, in that the aim of the study is to go beyond the behaviour exhibited in the classroom, to show how the Lakatosian and social theory of proof presented in chapter 5 can provide insight into students' notions of proof. Therefore the analysis of the transcripts I present in chapter 7 has as its focus what the students in the work group might "mean" by their utterances, and it interprets this meaning through the use of the theory.

6.7 Research design and method

6.7.1 Context and history

For practical reasons the group to be studied was selected by its choice of working area, which was in the quietest corner of the room. A cursory glance through the transcriptions of the students working in this group in a normal classroom environment shows that they do not engage in the abstract formulation of rigorous proofs. They make no ground-shaking discoveries, and both their final grades on the course and the content of their conversations suggest that they are somewhere between average and below average in mathematical ability. Nevertheless there are instances when they exhibit proof-like knowledge.

The Contexts and Strategies classroom was chosen for the investigation for two reasons. Firstly there was the practical consideration of convenience: I was one of the two lecturers teaching the course, and as was discussed in section 6.6 above, teacher based research is an established tradition in Mathematics Education. Secondly, the study was a continuation of previous research on students notions of proof (Finlow-Bates *et al.*, 1993; Finlow-Bates, 1994), which was conducted in the Contexts and Strategies classrooms of the previous two years, as detailed above. These studies suggested that students on the course were suitable for the investigation.

6.7.2 The topic and problems

For the purposes of my study it was important that the students had acclimatised to the new situations they were being exposed to, both locally within the environment of the Contexts and Strategies course, and globally with regards to the novel experiences of university life. Also, South Bank University has a significant problem with students dropping out in the initial weeks of the first semester, something which I fortunately knew of from the previous year's teaching, so to ensure that the group chosen would remain stable during the investigation it was necessary to wait at least four weeks. Secondly, it takes time for the students to establish effective group working strategies. Within these time limitations it was necessary to choose a topic in which the group would have opportunities to exhibit proof-like knowledge.

I decided to use the topic called Sequences and Series which the syllabus describes as follows (Winbourne and Finlow-Bates, 1993):

> Series and Sequences: Algebraic and geometric approaches to the generation and summation of series. Formal consideration of the notion of a limit. Foundations of calculus. (p.2)

The aim was for the students to examine converging, diverging and oscillating sequences and investigate the concept of a limit both informally and formally, through a set of structured worksheets, and for this to provide foundational knowledge for working with a variety of techniques for the summation of infinite series, guided by further worksheets. I selected the topic because I saw it as providing potential opportunities for the students to exhibit relevant behaviour. For example, the limits of sequences can be found through intuitive or experimental methods and verified using the formal definition of a limit. Series can be summed through informal visual methods and through more formal algebraic methods. There are also opportunities for justifying the methods used, and for the discovery of counter-examples to them.

6.7.3 Data collection

With regard to data collection, the decision needs to be made whether the observations are to be recorded and interpreted *in situ* through immediate coding, or whether the data should be collected on some other recording device and analysed retrospectively. Edwards and Westgate (1987) note that:

> Choice between instant coding and the various styles of retrospective analysis, then, reflects working assumptions about interaction and the transparency of talk, and about the kinds of data needed if the researcher is to capture more than the most unambiguously observed phenomena (who talked, most, and to whom). (p.57)

Furthermore, as Brodie (1994) observes:

> The use of recordings ... [allows] the words to be listened to repeatedly, and heard in the context of subsequent utterances and events as well as preceding ones. Only such an approach can begin to capture the meanings constituted in the interaction. (p.40)

There are significant disadvantages in retrospective analysis, namely that situational contexts and the dynamics of actually being there may be forgotten, especially if transcription of recordings takes place a considerable time later. However these disadvantages are more than outweighed by the intrusiveness of an observer in the situation of small group work, and the difficulties involved in developing a suitable coding scheme prior to the investigation.

Therefore the data was collected by using a small cassette recorder to audio-tape the group as they worked. In previous research (Finlow-Bates, 1994) I used a video tape recorder to film students in order to glean more data from, for example, the gestures and body language of the students as they were interviewed. In actuality, however, none of this extra data was of use. The physical practicalities of using a video camera (such as placing it in a suitable position in order to video all of the group participants) combined with its intrusive nature and the high probability that the extra information gained would be of little or no use suggested that the use of a cassette recorder would be sensible. The students in the group quickly became acclimatised to the presence of the cassette recorder, as evidenced by, for example, their occasional use of swearwords.

6.7.4 Transcription and coding

The transcription of the conversations recorded on the audio-cassettes presented several problems. Noise from the other groups working in the classroom was picked up, which sometimes obscured quieter speech from the group being studied. Secondly, the members of the group were prone to talking over each other, although fortunately the group rarely split up into sub-groups to discuss diverging interests. Repeatedly listening through the conversations has in some cases resolved both these types of ambiguity, but on rare occasions speech is simply lost. Finally, there were a few instances when it was not possible to attribute an utterance to one of the students, in which case the speaker was recorded as X. Barnes and Todd (1977, p.13) report similar difficulties with the transcription of audio tape recordings of small groups.

Although there are many transcription and coding schemes (see for example Edwards and Lampert, 1993) most appear to be biased towards meaning implied in the structure of the conversations, rather than with actual conversation content. This makes sense in the context of the origin of these coding schemes, derived as they are from linguistics, but for the purposes of a study in mathematics education they are likely to obscure rather than reveal what is going on. I have therefore resorted to a basic transcription procedure with a limited number of coding conventions. Exact lengths of pauses and details of intonation or speed of speech have been omitted except where relevant. For readability and clarity, verbally expressed formulae have been written down in a standard notation; thus for example the utterances "n to the power of two" and "n squared" are both recorded as "n^2". Finally, on the students' request, names have been consistently replaced by letters throughout the transcription.

Due to recording difficulties and the intrusion of classroom members external to the group being studied some of the classroom activities were not audio-taped and are therefore excluded from the transcriptions. These activities usually involved a plenary class review of the question being considered. As a result there are apparent discontinuities in the conversations and workings of the group. Where relevant, these are marked in the transcriptions. All activities specific to the group in question were however recorded.

6.7.5 Analysing the transcripts

Researchers such as Bell (1976) and Moore (1994) have analysed their data by explicitly categorising students' successes and, as their categories suggest is more often the case, their difficulties in dealing with proof, and then tabulating the results and presenting excerpts from the students' conversations or work to support particular hypotheses or models. On the other hand, authors such as Schoenfeld (1988), Reid (1995b), and to a certain extent Balacheff (1988, 1987) have taken the approach of providing only weakly defined categories, if at all, and relying primarily on illustrative quotations from the transcriptions. I have taken this latter approach, using the theory I have constructed to provide guidance in what to look for, and then using the transcriptions to provide an illustration of the theory in examining its usefulness.

In analysing transcripts of students working on proof, or in a situation with a potential for proving, my focus was on the meaning rather than the structure of the conversations taking place. I was not interested in identifying similarities or differences between specific instances of talk, or in providing quantified tables of results. Instead my initial analysis concentrated on instances when the group touched on any of the aspects of proof identified and discussed in chapter 3, "Aspects of proof", with the aim being to obtain insights into how the students engage with such aspects, and what role they play in the students' workings. I then re-examined the transcripts, searching for occasions when the students could be considered to have entered into hypothesis generation, either naïve or deductive, or into proofs and refutations style discussions. I was particularly interested in the social aspects of these two analyses, hoping to discover instances of the group developing their own protocols and methods of working through their interactions.

6.7.6 The report

Brodie (1994) identifies the importance of writing a report of qualitative research beyond that of communicating its results to other members of the academic community, when she states:

> It is in this process that the relationships between the data analysis and the theoretical framework in which it takes place are clarified. This is an essential part of an interpretive process which grounds explanation in the data. The theory informs the data analysis, which in turn informs the theory. (p.45)

This reveals a substantial difference between quantitative and qualitative research. In a quantitative study the research is usually finished when the writing up of the report starts, and the role of the report is to communicate the results of the research. In a qualitative study it is during the writing up that the links between theory and empirical evidence are explicated, and the research is refined.

In the next paragraph Brodie illustrates how the report fulfills the above role by continuing:

> Examples from the transcript and the pupils' written work are presented and analysed as part of the account. The examples that are chosen reflect important points in the development of the method and the pupils' knowledge, or exemplify key explanatory concepts. (p.45)

Given that the analysis and writing up are conducted by the researcher bringing his or her personal insight to bear on the data, the questions of reliability and validity of the research are the final points needing to be examined in this chapter. They are the topic of the next section.

6.8 Validity and reliability of the study

The concepts of validity and reliability of research originally arose within the positivistic paradigm of research (Brodie, 1994; Kaplan, 1989). Given the assumption that there are objective truths and generalisations to be discovered the question of to what extent the research has succeeded in unearthing such truths is a traditionally obvious one to ask. Within this context, research is described as valid if what the research intends to test or reveal is actually being tested for by the research methods. Reliability concerns how accurate the results of the research are, and to what extent the findings are generalisable. Within the tradition of qualitative research, however, objectivity is usually rejected, and the meanings, or even the relevance, of validity and reliability within such a context need to be reconsidered.

I intend to deal with the problems of validity and reliability in my study on two fronts. Firstly through the philosophical argument that positivistic research is misguided in its search for objectivity and thus suffers from the same weaknesses as qualitative research on this count. Secondly by the methodological argument that qualitative research can be construed as valid and reliable from its own standpoint, as endorsed by the community in which the research is to be disseminated.

As was previously noted, the questions of validity and reliability are closely linked with the idea of objectivity. It is on the basis of objectivity that I reconsider their role within a relativist qualitative study. Patton (1987) argues that: "... concerns about objectivity can often be better understood and discussed as concerns about neutrality" because "the neutral evaluator enters the field with no axe to grind, no theory to prove, and no predetermined results to support" (p.167). I dispute this evaluation for two reasons. Firstly, as has previously been stated, all research is based on explicit or implicit theoretical foundations, so the researcher cannot avoid having preconceptions about the results, and there will always be assumptions that cannot be refuted from within the theory. This does not establish these assumptions as unassailable eternally true facts. Secondly, what is considered neutral from one perspective may be seen as biased from another. This is as true for statistically unearthed conclusions as it is for more qualitative observations, for as Patton points out, "Numbers do not protect against bias; they sometimes merely disguise it" (p.166). So where now with validity and reliability?

Cohen and Manion (1994) identify two forms of validity which apply to experimental research, namely internal and external validity. Although experimental research lies within the positivistic paradigm, in that it attempts to statistically corroborate or refute hypotheses, the concepts of internal and external validity can be re-interpreted to form analogous concepts within the qualitative study. Internal validity can be related to consistency in the research, in that the methods used should bear a clear relation to the theory they are grounded in. External validity relates to justification and explication, in that it should be clear to the reader what the underlying assumptions of the research are, and to a reasonable extent why these assumptions have been adopted. Both forms of validity were attended to during the design and execution of the investigation.

To ascertain the level of reliability of the study is difficult. The observations were recorded from the interactions of four students: hardly a group of significant statistical size. However, I would argue that the relevance of reliability to the study is low except in the most conventional sense. Firstly it is not the aim of the study to produce statistically verified generalities; rather the aim is to illuminate the theoretical basis for proof constructed in the first half of the book by interpreting students' classroom behaviour in the light of it, and to observe its relevance and fruitfulness as a framework for this kind of study. Secondly, the fallibilistic nature of the theory underpinning the study suggests that any generalisations drawn from observations cannot be shown to be fundamentally reliable, they can only be corroborated or refuted by further observations.

6.9 Summary

The purpose of this chapter has been to provide a methodological basis for conducting an empirical investigation of a group of students working in a first year undergraduate mathematics classroom, in the light of the theoretical basis for proof constructed in the previous chapter. I have attempted to meet the aims of providing a sound methodology, and presenting and clarifying the links between the theoretical basis for proof and the investigation in the following ways:

- I have restated the theory of proof in the section "Scope and focus of the investigation" on page 114 in order to clarify the scope of the investigation and make its relation to the theory more explicit. The definition of a proof as a thought experiment coupled with a proof-analysis and the concept of mathematics as being quasi-empirical in nature are both considered to be key points in the report of the investigation, but the social dimension of the theory will not be examined in depth, primarily because this would widen the scope of the investigation to such an extent that the focus of the study on examining students' notions of proof would be lost.

- In the sections "Methodological issues" on page 116 and "A qualitative research methodology" on page 117, I argued that a qualitative research methodology is most suitable for the investigation. The reasons to support this included the following: the study has the natural setting of the mathematics classroom as its direct source of data, the report of the study is descriptive as opposed to quantitative or statistical, the investigation is concerned with proof as a process rather than proof as an outcome, and concepts such as "understanding" and "meaning" are paramount to the research.

- The section titled "Research design and method" on page 122 provided a background history of the Contexts and Strategies classroom, described the topic and worksheets being used during the investigation and gave details of the methods used for gathering and transcribing the data, and writing the report.

In the section "Validity and reliability of the study" on page 127, I addressed the problems of validity and reliability within my research as follows. Firstly, as far as possible, I tried to make explicit any theoretical assumptions adopted concerning the nature of proof and what it means to exhibit notions of proof. I have done this through a discussion of the quasi-empirical and social nature of proof in the first half of this book, and by reviewing other work within this area in mathematics education. Secondly I attempted to ensure the internal consistency of the research as far as possible through the selection of research methods relevant to the theory, research methods developed and tested over the course of the study. Due to the social nature attributed to proof in this case they consist of a qualitative analysis of transcriptions of a group of students working in a mathematics classroom. Finally I have, through the discussions contained in this chapter, attempted to present a considered justification of the methods used within my research.

7 Investigating students' notions of proof

7.1 Introduction

The students' work was guided by a series of worksheets, the aim of which was to introduce the topic of Sequences and Series, supported by some Open University materials (Open University, 1988). One of the aims of the sheets was to draw the students from initially informal definitions and investigations of sequences on to more formal considerations of the limit of a sequence. From there the students were to progress through a number of way of dealing with infinite series including a variety of visual approaches and an algebraic approach.

From the transcriptions one can see that the group was dedicated to working on the topic at hand — Sequences and Series. The students spent little time in idle conversation. From occasional jokes and humorous comments made to each other it appears that working in the Contexts and Strategies classroom was not considered overly onerous, which is pleasing considering the fact that each lesson was four hours long - a University policy. However what was disappointing was the generally low level of understanding evidenced in the students' work, although on many occasions they appeared to be heading in the right direction.

In this analysis of the transcriptions I have tried as far as possible to follow the group's work chronologically for two reasons: firstly for clarity, in that members of the group occasionally refer back to previous work, and secondly to reveal the manner in which the group's methods and protocols for working develop. I have also tried to avoid merely describing what the group was doing from one moment to the next unless it was necessary for an understanding of the processes taking place. As a result some of the more mundane activities of the group are not analysed.

7.2 Initial work on sequences

The aim of Sequences and Series sheet 1 is to provide the students with definitions of what a sequence is and to work on tasks such as producing a general rule or informally examining the limit of a variety of sequences. Because of this there are not many opportunities for the group to produce sophisticated proofs or thought experiments. However, there are numerous occasions where the group's conjecturing, corroboration and refuting activities can be examined, as well as their ability to deal with abstraction, generalisation, formal rules and definitions, all of which are relevant to students' abilities to produce proofs later on in the topic. As I will show, although the groups accuracy and level of mathematical sophistication remains low, the patterns of behaviour exhibited by the group develop along strongly Lakatosian lines.

7.2.1 Cycles of conjecture, refutation and corroboration

When working on the first set of questions on sheet 1, members of the group exclusively utilised naïve guessing to propose answers to the questions. Other members then put forward empirical evidence to either corroborate or refute the initial conjecture.

The first question concerns finding a general expression for the sequence 1, 2, 4, 8 ..., for which Phi proposes the following rule, described as follows:

> [Extract 1.1: tape 1, side A, lines 21-26]
>
> Phi: That's just doubling, isn't it?
> Delta: Yeah.
> (pause)
> Phi: So t(n) is equal to ... double the original thing.
> Mu: Why has it got 1 at the start then?
> Kappa: Yeah, that's what I was thinking.

The group is still coming to terms with what a sequence is, but already within the first few lines of conversation a conjecture has been put forward, followed quickly by a global refutation. The first problem with Phi's conjecture identified by Mu and Kappa is that the sequence on the worksheet starts with 1, whereas Phi's starts with 2. The group's discussion is hampered by the fact that Phi's conjecture is worded unclearly in English. The use of the word "thing" especially needs clarification. In the following extract, Mu interprets and refines the conjecture, and his refutation to it, by moving from a word description of the rule to an algebraic one, namely *2n*:

[Extract 1.2: tape 1, side A, lines 38-39]

Mu: Yeah, that one works because if you put 1 into that you get 1 out anyway. If you put 1 into 2n you don't get 1.

At this point the rest of the group, excepting Phi, consider the first conjecture laid to rest, and two new conjectures are put forward:

[Extract 1.3: tape 1, side A, lines 40-48]

Delta: 2^n?
Mu: Yeah. No ... n^2.
Kappa: Mmm ... n^2.
Mu: Or is it?
Phi: No, it's not n^2 because it's not squaring it.
Delta: No.
Phi: It's just doubling it.
Mu: 2^n.
Phi: (interrupts) It's 2n.

The group accepts Delta's original conjecture over Phi's after Delta provides empirical evidence for it, but the evidence raises a new question, namely which value of *n* constitutes a valid starting point for the sequence:

[Extract 1.4: tape 1, side A, lines 52-71]

Delta: 2^0 is 1.
Kappa: Oh yes, oh yes.
Delta: 2^0 is 1. 2^1 is 2. 2^2 is 4.
Mu: 2^n.
Delta: Yeah, 2^n.
Kappa: No it's not.
Delta: Why not?
Phi: 2^n.
Delta: Because 2^0 is 1, 2^2 is 2 ...
Mu: (speaking over Delta) But then you're starting at 0.
Delta: ... 2^2 is 4, 2^3 is 8, 2^4 is 16.
Kappa: Yeah, you're right.
Phi: 2^5 is 32.
Mu: But then you're starting at 0.
Delta: Yeah?
Kappa: Yeah, but that's all right, isn't it?

Mu: It's all right to start at zero?
Kappa: Yeah.
Delta: Yeah.
Mu: Well that's that.

Several important things occurred in the above extracts. Firstly a number of naïve conjectures were been put forward, only to be refuted by global counterexamples — the conjectures being $2n$ and n^2. Then 2^n was proposed and empirically corroborated. Finally Mu raised a refutation by questioning the fact that the 2^n conjecture required the counting of n to start at 0 instead of 1, but this refutation was overcome using monster-adjustment by Kappa, who argued that 0 was an acceptable starting point. Mu's counter-example is then no longer a counter-example, but becomes a corroborative example instead.

I take this to be a sign that the group is showing behaviour along the lines of Polya's and Lakatos' descriptions of naïve conjecturing through generalising and specialising. On the negative side, Phi has revealed another way of dealing with a refutation not listed by Lakatos: the method of counter-example-ignoring. It is only social pressure in the form of the rest of the group supporting Delta's conjecture that causes Phi to abandon his $2n$ conjecture and return to the discussion.

7.2.2 Transferal of knowledge about sequence starting points

In the above analysis the question of how the general rule for a sequence should relate to the natural numbers was raised. This is a question that the group continued to consider throughout their work on the first sheet. Recall that the initial conclusion drawn by the group was that "it's all right to start at 0". After having their first answer verified by lecturer W, they proceed to work on a general rule for the sequence 3/4, 4/5, 5/6, ... and the following conversation ensues:

[Extract 2.1: tape 1, side A, lines 113-124]

Kappa: Right, part b). (pause) um, n-1 on ... n-1/n, is it?
Phi: It's always going to be on n...
Mu: It's always going to be over n.
Delta: Yeah.
Phi: 8 over 9, etc.
Kappa: You write it down as n-1/n.

Mu: Yeah, oh yeah.
Kappa: Whether that's right, whether that's what we want ... I don't know.
Phi: I see what you mean. So if it was 9, it would be 9 - 1 ...
Kappa: 8. 8 over 9.
Phi: Yeah, that's basically it.
Kappa: Yeah.

The group appears to have more confidence about finding a general rule, as evidenced by the fact that one empirical test (Phi's "8 over 9, etc.") is considered sufficient to corroborate Kappa's conjecture. By line 123 all members of the group have voiced support for $n-1/n$ as the solution. However, at this point Mu initiates a new debate about sequence starting points:

[Extract 2.2: tape 1, side A, lines 125-135]

Mu: Shouldn't you start at 1/2, *i.e.* 1/2. And then it's 2/3 ...
Phi: We're having a bit of difficulty with the starting point, but then again, does the starting point matter? I don't know, do you just start from ...
Kappa: Yeah, I suppose it doesn't matter , so long ...
Phi: I mean, you could take each sequence back to anywhere, really, if you wanted to, but if the sequence starts ...
Delta: Go into negative numbers and stuff?
Phi: ... starts from there then I guess ...
Kappa: I think so long as the formula accounts for it, it will be all right.
Mu: Yeah.
Phi: So it would still work if you went from a half, or over it, wouldn't it?

It was Mu who originally questioned the starting point of sequences in extract 1.4, and although he seemed content with the answer offered at that time, it is interesting that within the context of a new question he feels the issue has been reopened. In response Phi, Kappa and Delta elaborate the question of starting points, which pacifies Mu. It is noteworthy, however, that Kappa's explanation, "so long as the formula accounts for it" which is a pragmatic approach implying that if "it works" then it must be all right, is different to Phi's "you could take each sequence back to anywhere" implying that the starting point is an arbitrary concept, and yet the combination of both is what appears to silence Mu's doubts. Delta's question, "Go into negative numbers and stuff?" suggests that the group might have been on the brink of an expansion of the concept of sequences, namely sequences that extend infinitely in both directions. This process of thought has had beneficial results to mathematics in the past; for example, an analogous investigation into series can lead to an abstraction from Taylor series to MacLaurin series.

135

However, the group chooses not to go in that direction. Instead, we observe the problem of sequence starting points arising a third time when W is reviewing the group's work. This time it is Phi who notices a discrepancy in the starting point of the sequence:

[Extract 2.3: tape 1, side A, lines 213-233]

W: ... All right, so let's have a look. What would the 100th term of that sequence be in b)?
Mu: 99/100.
W: 99/100. And what would the millionth term be?
Phi: Wouldn't it be over 104 or something because you're starting ...
W: Sorry?
Phi: ... from 3/4 so your 100th term...
W: Ah!
Phi: ... is going to be 103/104 or something like that.
W: OK, your formula doesn't say that, does it? According to your formula what is the first term?
Phi: If n was 104 ...
W: Yes?
Phi: ... then it would work, it would still be 103/104.
W: OK.
Phi: But our formula doesn't say that 3/4 is the first term.
W: No it doesn't. Could you adapt your formula to make it say that 3/4 was the first term?
Kappa: Umm...
(pause)
W: I mean, what are we taking n to be at the beginning?

W has not dictated what the answer should be, but the group's previously accepted assumptions are about to be disregarded in favour of the line of thinking that W helps Kappa and Phi follow:

[Extract 2.4, tape 1, side A, lines 239-254]

W: So you take the first n to be?
Kappa: 1.
W: The first term in the sequence: it makes sense. So you want the first term to be 3/4.
Kappa: Right.
W: Now, the first term as far as you have it at the moment if we substitute n=1 we get?
Phi: 1/2.
Kappa: Well, 0 over ...
W: You get 0/1 which is 0.
Phi: Yeah, OK, right.
W: Now you actually want 3/4.
Mu: Yes.
Kappa: So n has to be 4, no, 4.

W: Yeah, or perhaps you could change your description of it to make it 4th, your first, 3/4.

It is difficult to determine how much the group is achieving by itself here, and in particular how many of the conclusions drawn are those that W wants the group to adopt. For example, when Kappa suggests that the first *n* should be 1 in line 240, W offers considerable support, whereas when Kappa suggests that this should be changed in line 252, and that the counting of n should start from 4 to preserve the original formula of *n-1/n*, W offers a different suggestion. Given the authority invested in W as the course lecturer, it is not surprising that the group follows his route[1]:

[Extract 2.5. tape 1, side A, lines 256-267]

W: How do you get 3 from 1?
Kappa: Multiply by 3.
W: You could do. How else could you do it?
Kappa: Add 2.
W: Add 2. So you could ... how could you symbolise that?
(pause)
Kappa: Um, ... n+2, so the, n ...
W: Start with your n+2, that sounded fine to me. If that's the top one, what would the bottom one be?
Kappa: n+3.
Mu: Mmmm.
Phi: I get it, yeah.

With the help of W the group has now developed a method of adjusting a formula, describing a sequence, to start at *n=1*. The question remains as to whether the group will use this knowledge in the future, and therefore whether the definition as to what constitutes a correct formula for a sequence has been adopted. The following extract shows that this is indeed the case. In it, W leaves the group after pointing out that the group's answer to the first question, namely 2^n, has the same problem as above. The conversation proceeds as follows:

---

1 I am not trying to suggest that what W is doing here is wrong. As is usual in a classroom, there is a time limit and a syllabus to cover, and the class as a whole had previously exhibited a tendency to examine small differences in the group answers in great detail during plenary sessions, to the detriment of later work. By encouraging the groups to obtain similar answers on the first sheet, W is ensuring more time is made available to discuss significant differences on later sheets.

[Extract 2.6, tape 1, side A, lines 294-306]

(pause)
Kappa: So 2n-1 ...
(pause)
Kappa: Yeah, 2n-1.
Delta: Yeah.
Phi: n-1?
Kappa: Yeah. So if n is 1 ...
Kappa & Phi: ...it's 20
Kappa: which gives you ... 1.
Mu: Yeah, that's right.
Kappa: And then ...
Phi: The next one will be 21 ...
Kappa & Phi: 21 which is 2. Yeah.

In the above extracts we see the group encountering an issue not explicit in the worksheet; the question of how a general formula for a sequence should relate to the natural numbers. Individuals provide different reasons in the face of questioning by other members of the group to justify why they have put forward particular answers to the worksheet questions. For example, Phi argues that the starting point of a sequence was arbitrary in line 129 when questioned, and Kappa provides a pragmatic reason in line 133. Finally, with the guidance of one of the lecturers, the group tries out a particular strategy for dealing with the problem, namely assuming that counting with *n* starts at 1 and adjusting their formulas accordingly. Extract 2.6 provides evidence, through the transferral of the strategy to a previous problem, that they have, for the moment at least, adopted this strategy as an assumption about sequences.

7.2.3 An attempt at an exhaustive analysis of $t(n) = a^n$

After a plenary session in which all the groups in the classroom compare their answers to questions a) - j) on sheet 1, the groups are set to work on the second question on sheet 2, which consists of investigating the behaviour of $t(n)=a^n$ for different values of *a*. The aim of this question is to ensure that each group forms a good intuitive understanding of the concept of a limit before proceeding on to examine its formal definition. In this study question 2 offers the opportunity to examine how the group reasons about a problem requiring an exhaustive and therefore probably systematic examination of the properties of an infinite set of sequences.

The group starts working on the question immediately and chooses *a*=0 for its first point of inquiry:

[Extract 3.1, tape 1, side B, lines 13-16]

Kappa: Right, a is 0. 0 to the power of anything.
Mu: I thought we're starting at 0.
Kappa: 0 to the power of ... 0 is 0.
Phi: 0.

From listening to the tapes it seems that Kappa is not talking about 0^0 (which is an undefined quantity). Instead, when he states that "0 to the power of ... 0 is 0" the emphasis is on the second half, "0 is 0", whereby I assume he means "when *a* = 0 the limit is 0". Apart from the emphasis heard on the tape this interpretation is supported by the dialogue on lines 63-66 in extract 3.3 with Kappa agreeing with Phi.

As the conversation continues the group members identify what they initially believe constitutes all possible cases. They classify the type of sequences produced according to whether *a* is negative, zero, between zero and one, or greater than one:

[Extract 3.2, tape 1, side B, lines 17-33]

Kappa: If a is a negative number, then it's going to be a positive or a negative. No, it's going to be a positive.
(pause)
M (quietly): We've still got another hour.
Kappa: It is 0, right, and you get 0. If a is a negative number then you can get either negative equality or positive equality. If a is a decimal, a small ...
Mu: Tend to 0, won't it?
Kappa: That's it, it would be, it would tend to 0, wouldn't it? Um.
Phi: If it's greater than 1 then um ...
Kappa: Not quite, 0.0001 to the power, say 100, equals ... 0.0001^{100} =, yep, tends to 0.
Phi: So if it's in-between 0 and 1?
Kappa: It tends to 0, otherwise ...
Phi: Above 1 it goes off to infinity.
Kappa: Yep.
Mu: Sorted.
Kappa: Sorted!

The group is not demonstrating a systematic search pattern in answering the question, and so appears still to be relying on naïve guessing as its conjecture origination method. However, Kappa does exhibit a more informed choice for empirical investigation by selecting a small positive *a* and a large *n* when trying to refute or corroborate Mu's hypothesis that for small positive *a*, *t(n)* tends to 0. This choice corroborates Mu's conjecture.

Having talked about the various cases for *t(n)*, Kappa suggests that the group should try and write down their conclusions. During this process the group discovers another case, namely *a*=1, and includes it in their write-up:

[Extract 3.3, tape 1, side B, lines 61-72]

Phi: Oh, if it's 1 as well, we didn't put if it is 1. Hmm. If it is 1 it stays ...
Kappa: 1^{100} is 1. Yeah.
Phi: Well, just 1 to the ... 1 will always be 1.
Kappa: Yeah.
Phi: Just as 0 to the ... 0 will always be ...
Kappa: Yeah. n = 1, then ...
Mu: Do you understand that?
Phi: Yeah. Just about.
Kappa: ... equals ... uh, a = 1, a = 1 ... a = 0 ... = 0.
Phi: That's it, isn't it?
Kappa: Yeah.
Phi: I can't find any more limits from a, really.

I find it interesting that although Phi expresses surprise at finding another distinct case for which *t(n)* has a different limit, neither Phi nor any other member of the group takes this as an indication that there may be even more cases they have missed, nor does it seem to have engendered any desire to ensure the completeness of their answer.

A short while later W joins the members of the group to see how they have been doing. He causes them to review their answers, in particular their written answer for a being negative. When he leaves the group he gives them the following instructions:

[Extract 3.4, tape 1, side B, lines 121-126]

W: So now you need to write that succinctly, and agree between you what you're going to say so you can capture everything.
Kappa: OK.
Phi: What, one in plain English and ...
W: And you can volunteer it as a group in about 2 minutes. Eh, two minutes, and we'll get back together. That's all I think it needs.

I am not sure what Phi means by "one in plain English", but I think he is asking if the group's notation should be in English rather than in an algebraic form. However, W's words do prompt the group into a closer examination of their answers, which were written down in an unordered manner before. This second review causes Phi to notice something new:

[Extract 3.5, tape 1, side B, lines 151-155]

Phi: What happens if it's between 0 and -1?
Mu: That's what I was just thinking.
Kappa: 0.0001 minus.
Mu: It'll tend to ... it'll still tend to 0, wouldn't it?
Kappa: Negative.

Kappa's comment of "Negative" is directed at Phi, to get him to enter a negative number into his calculator. It is not a denial of Mu's conjecture. A new case for *t(n)* has been discovered by writing the answers to the question down in an ordered manner.

Immediately after this, Phi indicates that he has refined the group's method of empirical investigation for examining the limit of a sequence:

[Extract 3.6, tape 1, side B, lines 156-160]

Phi: Hopefully yeah, where, where is your negative on this Crimean war job[2]?
Kappa: Just plus minus negative inverse to the power try 3 first, then try square as well.
Phi: Try a big number ... mmm ... zero. There you go. If it's between 0 and -1 or 0 and 1 ...

Kappa's cryptic instructions are to Phi, suggesting that he should try to cube their trial number, which is still -0.0001 (see extract 3.5). However, Phi has different plans. His strategy involves trying "a big number" for *n*. To use Mason's (1980) terminology, he is showing an effective use of specialisation. Recall also Kappa's initial choice of +0.0001 as a number close to 0 in extract 3.2. Compared to the *ad hoc* manner in which members of the group were selecting empirical examples when working on the first sheet (for example the arbitrary choice of *n* = 9 in extract 2.1) the group is showing a marked increase in sophistication in their naïve guessing strategies.

The above examination causes Phi, Mu and Kappa (Delta appears to have left the group half an hour before) to reduce three cases, namely 1 < *a* < 0, *a* = 0 and 0 < *a* < 1 into one case:

---

2   He is talking about Kappa's calculator.

[Extract 3.7, tape 1, side B, lines 162-167]

Mu: So can't you just say ..
Kappa: Greater than -1.
Mu: If it's between -1 and 1 it tends to 0. It's the same isn't it?
Phi: Yeah, yeah you can put it that way, you can put it -1 to 1 I suppose, instead of doing the two different ones.
Kappa: Yeah, right, we can do that. OK.

and further on,

[Extract 3.8, tape 1, side B, lines 176-180]

Kappa: So you don't even have to say a to, a = 0. That's clearly it.
Phi: Yeah, that's the point. If, if you're going from -1 to 1 then when it gets to 0 it's 0. Well, then if it's , its, its in-between there, anyway, it's tending to 0 'cause it's all tending to 0.
Mu: Yeah.

Having taken a general problem and specialised it into a number of cases, the group is now involved in a kind of generalising to reduce the number of cases. They have achieved this by regarding the important part of the behaviour of *t(n)* as *n* tends to infinity to be its limit, rather than other properties such as oscillation or the rate of convergence to the limit.

Finally, at the end of the transcription of tape 1, side B we are left with a tantalising fragment of conversation when Phi asks if there is a reason for the sequences behaving as they do:

[Extract 3.9, tape 1, side B, lines 195-202]

Phi: a is greater than 1 ... then ... which is (unclear) equal to ... is there any reasoning for this? Wait a minute.
Kappa: Well there is ...
Phi: Whatever, does anyone have a reason for this?
Kappa: Uhu.
Delta: If n < -1 ...
W: OK!
Kappa: Right, let's just turn this off.

This is the first time a member of the group asks a deeper question indicating a desire to know "why" rather than just asking questions concerned with the surface level of the problem at hand. Unfortunately W's shout of "OK!" signalled the final plenary session for the class before the end of the lesson. What reasoning, if any, the group would have come up with to justify their answers remains a mystery.

To summarise, this section of the analysis is concerned with the group's conjecture forming strategies. Unsurprisingly there are no deductively formed conjectures. However, during the process of working on the sequence problems the group show an improvement in their techniques for empirically corroborating their guesses, by informed specialization. Furthermore, by focusing only on the property of limits the group successfully generalises three similar cases in the final problem into one encompassing description.

7.3 A formal investigation of limits

Tape 2 marks the start of a new classroom session. By this time it was assumed that the members of the group would be used to working with each other and would be familiar with basic sequence concepts. The first task of the day was to make sense of the formal definition of a limit[3]. In the extracts we see the group working with two sequences, $t(n)=n+2/n+3$ and $t(n)=\sqrt{(n+1)}-\sqrt{(n)}$. There are two points to focus on at this point of the analysis. Firstly the group is trying to make sense of a formal definition, hence we see the first occurrence of the group trying to work in a more formal rather than intuitive manner. Secondly we see the first clear opportunity for the group to engage in what mathematicians might regard as proving. Previously the group had postulated conjectures concerning the limits of two sequences but now they are in a position to "confirm" those conjectures using the formal definition. This confirmation can take the form of a proof.

From a lecturer's point of view I find that the behaviour exhibited by the group is, on the whole, encouraging. The transcripts have revealed that numerous successful attempts were made by the group in approaching the questions, many of which I was unaware of during the class. There were also some disappointing occurrences, particularly when the group came close to completing questions only to fail at the last hurdle. On the positive side the group tried out several interesting avenues in applying the definition whilst trying to prove their conjectures concerning the limits of the two sequences. Barring some algebraic errors and difficulties with some of the manipulations the groups succeeded fairly well. On the negative side there were occasions where the

---

3 A sequence $t(n)$ has limit L if, given any $e>0$ there is some natural number N so that $|L-t(n)|<e$ whenever $n>N$.

indication was that some of the members of the group were not really sure why they were dealing with the definition, and what its significance was.

7.3.1 *Making sense of the definition*

Having seen a demonstration of the formal definition applied to a sequence to prove its limit, the group decides to work on the sequence $t(n)=n+2/n+3$, for which they previously conjectured that the limit was 1. Then they start to look at the definition in relation to their chosen sequence:

[Extract 4.1, tape 2, side A, lines 28-38]

Kappa: What have we got to do?
Delta: We've got to ... we've got to ... no idea. What have we got to do?
Phi: I don't know.
Kappa & Phi: What's a) for?
Kappa: The limit 's 1, isn't it?
Delta: You're doing question b)?
Phi: Ah, yeah. You've got to do it in the same form as this. You've got to find out N.
Kappa: We ... oh ... when ... for what value of epsilon we need another value for ...
Delta: Well, go ... do 1 first and do 0 later.

Phi has tried to summarise the essence of the definition in lines 34 and 35. Together with Kappa he seems be coming to grips with the definition very quickly. The group continues to discuss how to proceed:

[Extract 4.2, tape 2, side A, lines 40-47]

Delta: You can, you can, ah, epsilon at 0.
Kappa: You could have a value very close to negative ...
Mu: That's 1 isn't it? Remember this one.
Phi: Yeah. You have to use ...
Kappa: Use an epsilon of 0.01.
Delta: No, you don't want to go to hard into it. Just do a nice epsilon.
Phi: 0.1. Yeah.
Kappa: That then. Yeah.

The above extract and the one before it demonstrate that the group realises the key is to find N given an epsilon, although I am not convinced they know why this is the case. As is usual, they decide to try out an example. The group has learned from previous cases that it is best to start out simple and build up from there. However Delta, by talking about an "epsilon at 0" appears to be harbouring a suspicion that if epsilon is taken to be 0, then "the answer" will drop out somehow. He brings this point up somewhat later and is supported by Mu:

[Extract 4.3, tape 2, side A, lines 75-80]

Delta: Then you've got to do it when it's 0 to find the value of N, isn't it?
Phi: Pardon?
Delta: You've got to do it when it's 0 ...
Mu: Yeah.
Delta: ... to find the value of N.
Mu: Yeah.

However, Kappa and Phi ignore Delta's interpretation of what to do, and being the more dominant members of the group their disinterest causes Delta's ideas to be forgotten. Although in this case this is fortunate for the group, it is interesting that decisions concerning which avenues to explore often appear to be reached along social lines rather than on the basis of a refutation or an informed argument. This has its counterpart in the mathematics community, where topics and investigations are sometimes identified as being "of interest to the community" on the basis of the academic standing of their proponent rather than the merit of the work itself. Of course there is always the possibility that Kappa and Phi silently refuted Delta's suggestion but did not deign to inform the group.

After a moment of confusion when the group's discussion dissolves into chaos, Kappa starts writing down an inequality which will form the basis of the group's future work on the problem of limits:

[Extract 4.4, tape 2, side A, lines 96-99]

Kappa: 0.9 is less than t(n) ...
Delta: So you do it then?
Phi: Let me start with some numbers and I'll put the sequence through it.
Kappa: ... which is less than 1.1.

The class had previously been shown that the inequality in the formal definition, $|L-t(n)| < e$ could be rewritten as $L-e < t(n) < L+e$, which explains what Kappa is writing down.

After Kappa writes down his inequalities, Delta verbalises some of his thoughts, which show that he has understood the mechanics of the definition of a limit:

[Extract 4.5, tape 2, side A, lines 109-115]

Delta: You do it to work out the value of N, isn't it?
Kappa: Yeah.
Delta: Doubtless, I thought, because you've worked that ... that's the limit, that bit there. That's your limit, isn't it?
Kappa: Yes.
Delta: That's what you've already worked out.
Phi: Uhu.

The observations in lines 109, 111 and 114 indicate that Delta has surmised that the limit is known before the definition is applied, and that the definition verifies the limit in hindsight. It is interesting that the usual problem, where students do not see the point of proving a theorem if they are already convinced of its truth, does not seem to apply here. This could be because the group has a sense of the relevance the definition of a limit. It could also be that they are simply going through the motions to satisfy the course requirements.

7.3.2 *Proving that the limit of t(n) = n+2/n+3 is 1*

In the previous extracts the group was trying to make sense of the formal definition by starting to apply it to one of the sequences they were working on in the previous class, for which they had conjectured a limit of 1. From these initial steps they drew conclusions concerning how to apply the definition to show that their conjecture was indeed correct. These conclusions were of a general nature ("You've got to find out *N*" in line 36, "That's your limit ... that's what you've already worked out" in lines 114 and 112). In this section we see the group trying to work with the algebra of the definition to complete their proof.

Mu and Delta continue to flesh out the original inequalities. By then end of the following extract Delta has verbalised an equation deduced, as suggested by his use of the word "implies", from the application of the definition of a limit to the problem the group is working on:

[Extract 5.1, tape 2, side A, lines 122-129]

Mu: So you should put n+2/n+3 in there ...
Delta: ... in the middle ...
Phi: Yeah, well that's n .... isn't it.
Delta: As in, work it out like that.
Mu: The limit will be, well it'll be 1 minus that won't it, instead of 0.

Delta: Yeah, 1. Yeah, 'cause the limit there was 3.
Phi: Yeah, you've got 1 minus, so it'll be 1 minus ... n plus ...
Delta: It implies 1 minus epsilon, solves, is n+2/n+3 then plus absolute value.

Notice that the group has moved from the specialised consideration of epsilon as 0.1 to the generalised consideration of epsilon as an unknown. They continue to shift back and forth from this specialization in the work that follows, although I have been unable to detect a pattern in this shifting.

After writing down the inequalities which reduce the problem into manageable pieces, Delta and Kappa notice something they consider to be so important that it needs mentioning several times, namely that the elements of the sequence can never be greater than 1:

[Extract 5.2, tape 2, side A, lines 138-140]

Delta: If it's, if it's ... it is ... 'cause if it's equal to 1 the answer can't be less than 1 ... it can't be more than 1 can it?
Kappa: That's right, yeah. That's right, yeah.

and

[Extract 5.3, tape 2, side A, lines 145-146]

Delta: So it can't be more than 1 so it's tending to 1.
Kappa: Mmm.

and finally

[Extract 5.4, tape 2, side A, lines 150-152]

Kappa: 1 is the limit. It can't be more than 1.
Delta: It can't be more than 1.
Kappa: Yeah.

We have reached the point where the problem the group is dealing with can be broken down into a "proof-like" thought-experiment and a proof-analysis in a Lakatosian manner. Although they have not written each stage down explicitly, what follows is my interpretation of the thoughts that the group has verbalised, discussed and ordered according to the Lakatosian theory of proof developed in chapter 5:

Conjecture: The limit of $t(n) = n+2/n+3$ is 1.

This conjecture was first made explicitly by the group in lines 21 to 32 of tape 2, side A.

<u>Thought-experiment</u>: If the above conjecture satisfies the formal definition of a limit then it is true.

In a sense the definition lies at the core of the thought-experiment, and thus it is difficult to determine to what level the group is working with it. I also recognise that there may be different interpretations of what constitutes a thought experiment in this context. For example, when I work with the definition I view it as an algorithm or a machine, through which a sequence is passed, and depending on the outcome my conjecture as to the limit of the sequence is refuted or corroborated. The validity of the definition is not in question during this process — it forms the subject of a different inquiry. From the transcripts it is not clear how the group thinks about the definition, although there is evidence that the members of the group have an understanding of its workings (see for example, extract 4.5). Given the readiness with which the group applies the definition to their sequence I would conjecture that they have adopted a similar unquestioning approach during their work.

<u>Proof-analysis</u>:

1. The formal definition of a limit is the correct definition of a limit to use in this instance.

    This lemma is not explicitly stated by the group, and can therefore best be regarded as a hidden lemma. I include it because falsification of the definition of a limit would constitute a local counterexample to the proof, and in the Contexts and Strategies course of the year before a typographical error in the definition resulted in exactly this occurrence. The fact that the group works with the given definition indicated that they are relying on this lemma, albeit unwittingly.

2. Using the definition in the case of $t(n)$ means that we are looking for a natural number N such that:

    $1 - e < n+2/n+3 < 1 + e$ for any $e > 0$ and any $n > N$.

    This particular casting of the definition of a limit was given to the group during a plenary session, and was corroborated by the class. The group verbalises this lemma in extract 4.4, as was previously discussed.

3. We do not need to consider the second half of the

inequality in lemma 2, because $n+2/n+3$ can never be bigger than 1.

This is the lemma Delta and Kappa were verbalising in extracts 5.2 to 5.4, for example when Delta states "So it can't be more than 1 so it's tending to 1" in line 145, tape 2, side A.

4. Therefore N is found by substituting N for n in the equation in lemma 2, *i.e.* by solving

$1 - e < N+2/N+3$

and choosing an N that satisfies this inequality. Evidence that the group is considering this lemma of the proof-analysis is given in the continuation of their discussion below.

Kappa repeats the inequality in lemma 4, but with epsilon taken as 0.1. This is the first of a number of occurrences when the group shifts from the general to the specific when working on what I have identified as lemma 4:

[Extract 5.5, tape 2, side A, lines 163-170]

Kappa: So 0.9 is less than n+2/n+3.
Mu: Yeah it's equal to that.
Phi: Hm.
Delta: Where'd you get the 0.9 from.
Kappa: Because, uh (simultaneous with Phi) 1 minus 0.1
Phi: 1 minus 0.9. Whereas in the other one it's 1 plus (drowned out by Kappa)
Kappa: 1 minus epsilon. Which is ... epsilon is 0.1.
Phi: That, this bit here is 0.9, anyway.

Kappa and Phi in particular here seem to be happier working on equations with only one unknown. Recall that Delta previously wrote down the general inequality for this problem (extract 4.6), namely $1 - e < n+2/n+3$. As the following extract shows, Phi's reluctance to deal with a general epsilon may be more a question of confidence rather than a lack of knowledge about how to deal with inequalities containing two unknowns:

[Extract 5.6, tape 2, side A, lines 172-174]

Phi: We could have gone for a challenge here ... epsilon 0.0001 what you like.
Delta: I thought we were doing the general rule that's, that was ...
Phi: Well, yeah, I mean you can't have generally ... but then you can just mmm ...

Delta still wants to work on the "general rule". Phi on the other hand wants to use a specific value for epsilon, but shows that he recognises that epsilon can take any value ("epsilon 0.0001 what you like"). He does however seem to contradict himself in the final sentence, which could mean that he does not fully understand the definition of a limit and considers epsilon in the inequality to be a particular, rather than a general quantity. By this I mean that whereas the definition requires an *N* to be found given any epsilon, Phi could be interpreting it to mean that an *N* is to be found given an epsilon. The distinction is crucial to understanding the definition, although it appears on the surface to be minimal.

The group are close to proving that 1 is indeed the limit for $t(n) = n+2/n+3$), as all they need to do is solve $1 - e = N+2/N+3$ and write everything up clearly and succinctly. However, solving this equation turns out to pose significant difficulties. The original aim, to prove that the limit of *t(n)* is 1 becomes obscured by a subgoal; solving the equation in lemma 4.

Delta suggests copying the method of an example on the board, in which logs were used[4]:

[Extract 5.7, tape 2, side A, lines 178-188]

Delta: Do it like that ... mmm ... hey, logs, isn't it? Logs, ln ...
Mu: You don't need to take logs for this one ...
Delta: Yes you do.
Mu: ... 'cause there's no powers, is there?
Delta: You can still take logs, though.
Phi: Hmm.
Mu: No?
Delta: 'Cause then you can do like that ...
Phi (simultaneously): I thought you need logs for the powers.
Mu: Are you saying that's to the power of -1?
Delta: No, you do it like that.

Delta remains convinced that the equation can be solved using logs despite Mu and Phi's comments to the effect that logs are used to solve equations involving powers. Then Mu tries to solve the equation using simple algebra, but runs into problems which

---

4   The example on the board concerned finding the limit of the sequence $t(n) = 2^n$, and went something like this:
$1/(2^N) = e$
$2^N = 1/e$
$\ln(2^N) = \ln(1/e)$
therefore $N = \ln(1/e)/\ln(2)$

Delta takes as ammunition in support of his "use logs" hypothesis:

[Extract 5.8, tape 2, side A, lines 192-200]

Mu: Yeah, but you don't need to do that, do you? See, you can just multiply that into that.
Kappa: Yeah.
Mu: Ah.
Delta: Then, but, but if you multiply it out you're still going to be left with that, that cancelled out ... there's no way you can do it.
Mu: Yeah, but how can you do it like that then?
Delta: That's what I'm trying to work out now.
Mu: Oh.

I believe the problem Mu has encountered in multiplying $1-e = N+2/N+3$ out is that he has obtained $N+3-eN-3e = N+2$ and cannot see how to reduce this to an equation with N on one side and e on the other. Both Delta and Mu do however recognise that separating the variables is the aim here:

[Extract 5.9, tape 2, side A, lines 202-206]

Mu: Can't you times that by say ... uh ... you want to get rid of one of those n's, don't you. Times it by ...
Delta: Could you do it like that?
(pause)
Mu: Yeah, but you've just got to get it on its own, haven't you?

and

[Extract 5.10, tape 2, side A, lines 231-232]

Delta: 'Cause you've got to factorise in such a way ... that you only get n as a factor.

Throughout the discussion Delta hopes that by using logs, the problem of separating the variables will somehow be solved. Mu tries to convince him that $\ln(x)$ does not have the properties he hopes it does:

[Extract 5.11, tape 2, side A, lines 216-221]

Delta: Can't you times out ... if you do ln inside the bracket ... like, times it out.
Mu: I don't think so. I don't know.
Delta: That's what you said.
Mu: Yeah, but if you've got sin 5, eh, sin 6x, you don't have sin 2x plus sin 4x.
Delta: Yeah, but we're talking about ln here.
Mu: I know, but it's just the same, really.

Mu is trying to draw an analogy between the familiar function $\sin(x)$ and the unfamiliar function $\ln(x)$, to convince Delta that logs will not help him to solve the equation. Delta remains unconvinced until Mu discovers a new way to deal with the inequality which looks promising, thereby distracting the group away from the logs approach. The new method uses partial fractions:

[Extract 5.12, tape 2, side A, lines 245-252]

Mu: That's right, I think I've got it now.
(loud noise of papers being shuffled)
Mu: Yeah, that's it, look. You've got n+2/n+3, yeah.
Group: Uhu.
Mu: That's just the same as saying n+3-1 at the top, yeah. So now you can separate, can't you, so you've got n+3 over n+3 minus 1 over n+3. That's just 1, so you get that and you've just got one n. Terrific
(relieved laughter)

So far it is has not been the students' proof-knowledge that is letting them down, it is their difficulties with algebra. This supports the idea that difficulties encountered by students when engaging in proving can be due to a lack of understanding of the content rather than a lack of understanding of proof.

Mu's inspired step may help the group solve the equation and find a solution for N. However, first he has to explain to them what he has achieved. Firstly Mu tries to go through his workings with Kappa, Phi and Delta:

[Extract 5.13, tape 2, side A, lines 253-263]

Kappa: n+2/n+3 is n+3 ...
Phi: (unclear) how you did that.
Kappa: -1/n+3 which is n+3 ...
Mu: minus 1 over n+3.
Phi: That's right, that is.
Delta: That's right.
Mu: And that is equal to 1 - 1/n+3 ...
Kappa: No, 'cause this is equal to 1 over 1, not 1 over n+3 is it?
Mu: Yeah. No, I'm talking about if you separate this, like you've go that bit there.
Kappa: All right, yeah.
Mu: And that bit there, see.

Although the group claims to be convinced, they all sound hesitant on the tapes, and it is not surprising that Mu proceeds to resort to the usual method of convincing the group. He provides them with an empirical example:

[Extract 5.14, tape 2, side A, lines 266-280]

Mu: And it just goes down to that. If you put numbers in you can just try it with numbers, like ... say we've got 3/4, you get 1 minus 1/1, is that right?
Phi: 1/1?
Delta: 4.
Kappa: 4.
Phi: Where'd you get the 1/4?
Mu: n+3. So if you just use n as 1, yeah, yeah?
Group: Yeah.
Mu: So it's 1 - a quarter which is 3 over 4. If you do n equal to 2, which is 4/5, so 1 minus 1/5 is ... it's right!
Kappa: All right, yeah, that sounds good to me.
Phi: Well, I'm still confused.
Mu: OK.
(pause)
Phi: mmm ... 1 - 1/7 ... OK.

Mu presents the group with two empirical examples, followed by the exclamation, "it's right!". Phi needs to try one further example himself before he is convinced. Once again the empirical method is favoured over the deductive method for gaining conviction.

Mu has now convinced the group to add a fifth lemma to the proof-analysis, providing a further step towards a complete proof that the limit of t(n) is 1:

   5. $N+2/N+3$ is equal to $1 - 1/(N+3)$.

I have listed this lemma as 5, although it could equally be viewed as a sub-lemma of lemma 4 in the proof-analysis given at the end of the previous section. The decomposition of a conjecture into a proof-analysis does not need to proceed along linear lines, which is an advantage this perspective of proof has over the idea of proof as simply a logical chain of argument.

7.3.3 The final stage of the proof

After Mu's observation has been accepted W comes over to see how the group is doing. He supports Mu's method of working over Delta's suggestion to use logs, which results in the group following Mu's line of investigation. They also explain to W why they are only looking at one side of the inequality (lemma 3). During this explanation the equation they are looking at is described in terms of epsilon as a general variable, rather than a specific number substituted for epsilon. This marks yet another point where the group moves from the specific (remember that epsilon had been chosen to be 0.1 previously) to the general.

After W leaves the group quite some time (lines 333-440) is spent trying to rearrange the equation to separate N from epsilon. The final result is as follows:

[Extract 6.1, tape 2, side A, lines 441-444]

Mu: Divide by epsilon. So you get 1/epsilon. You've got n plus 3 on this side. Then just minus the 3.
Phi: So N is equal to 1/epsilon minus 3. Well, no, if epsilon's .1, 1/.1 is 10, so N is 7.

It is difficult to tell from the tapes whether a speaker is talking about "N" or "n", so for the purposes of this analysis I have tried to make an educated guess in each case. In the above extract Mu has finally solved the equation correctly to obtain a formula from which N can be calculated given any epsilon. Phi then works out N given an epsilon of 0.1. However, the group makes a significant error when interpreting the equation solved above in terms of an inequality, which is explained after this extract:

[Extract 6.2, tape 2, side A, lines 445-455]

Mu: It's um ... so epsilon is less than it. Oh no, it is that less than?
Phi: Pardon?
Mu: Is that less than?
Phi: Yeah.
Mu: Yeah.
Phi: N is less than ... 7.
Mu: N is less than 7 for epsilon is equal to 0.1.
Kappa: 6.
Phi: Hm?
Kappa: So epsilon would be, no, so N would be 6.
Phi: Well, that's kind of equal to or less isn't it, something like that?

In the process of evaluating $1 - e < N+2/N+3$ they have multiplied both sides of the inequality by -1, but have failed to reverse the inequality sign. Therefore their solution is incorrect. The fact that they fail to notice that the test of their answer shows it to be wrong could be taken to mean that they have not fully understood the formal definition of a limit. On the other hand the group has spent a long time working on the question, and the relief of having obtained an answer may have caused them not to question its validity too closely. What is certain however, is that the group believe they have finished with the question, although a certain amount of discontent with the answer is evident:

[Extract 6.3, tape 2, side A, lines 466-467]

Delta: All I've done is piddle around with stupid (unclear).
Mu: At least we've finished with g). That's all right.

As a lecturer one might be tempted somewhat hastily to criticise the group's mathematics. However, from a researcher's point of view the above exchange was fruitful. Over the course of the above analysis the group proposed a conjecture and developed a detailed proof-analysis in an attempt to prove this conjecture, although they were probably unaware that they have been engaged in proving. It is true that there exists a simple local counterexample or refutation to their proof. However it is important to remember that as a mathematically experienced observer it is easy to notice the flaws in the group's work. A similar charge may be levelled at current advanced mathematics as it is probable that there are "obvious" refutations to proofs which are currently accepted as correct. Finally, it is important to notice that the pattern of working exhibited by the group can be meaningfully interpreted in the light of the theory developed in this investigation, regardless of the accuracy of the group's actual answers.

7.3.4 *Proving that the limit of t(n) = √(n+1) - √n is 0*

Believing that they have finished applying the definition of a limit to question b) on sheet 1, the group proceeds to work on h). What is immediately noticeable from the transcripts is that the group is now much more familiar with the procedure for proving what the limit of a sequence is. In the above analysis it took the group about 400 lines of transcription to get to lemma 5, whereas for question h) they reach the same point in about 40 lines.

Some of the members of the group are also beginning to show a significant development of proof knowledge. Kappa, for example, makes the following observation about the role of epsilon in the definition:

[Extract 7.1, tape 2, side A, lines 487-491]

Delta: What epsilon do we use to start with?
Kappa: Well, lets just not bother with it for now, I think.
Delta: What's that?
Kappa: Just use the symbol, just to get a formula. 'Cause we didn't use an epsilon last time did we?

This shows that Kappa has really comprehended the generality of the formal definition of a limit, namely that an *N* needs to be found given any epsilon. Delta is still not happy with this though, and wants to substitute a specific value for epsilon. Kappa agrees, but for a different reason than Delta. He wishes to see which of the two inequalities is relevant for the problem:

[Extract 7.2, tape 2, side A, lines 492-497]

Delta: We've got to use that to make sure ... to find its value...
Kappa: Yeah yeah yeah yeah. Yeah yeah. To see which side of the equation to use.
Mu: We might as well just use 0.1.
Delta: 0.1?
Phi: Yeah, 0.1 will be all right, yeah. What is it this time? Goes to 0.

Once again the group resolves the problem as to which half of the inequality to use in their proof within twenty lines (given that Kappa raised the question in the above extract on line 493) as can be seen in the following two extracts:

[Extract 7.3, tape 2, side A, lines 503-504]

Delta: And we use the positive side.
Phi: And then 0 and then ...

and

[Extract 7.4, tape 2, side A, lines 511-513]

Phi: Hm. t(n) using this side, I think. Can't be this side can it? So it's basically root of n + 1 minus the root n is ... um ... less than 0.1.
Kappa: Yeah, it's going to be the right hand side of these ...

The group has reached the point where algebra stands between them and a proof of the conjecture that the limit of $\sqrt{(n+1)} - \sqrt{n}$ is 0. It is worth noting here that the group has transferred the method developed on question b) successfully and quickly, and in the process they have spent much less time debating whether the conclusions drawn are correct or not. An increased level of familiarity with the type of question, the routinisation of some of the procedures used in answering the questions, and an increased level of confidence in their abilities due to what the group perceives as a successful completion of previous questions may all play a part in this.

The group recognises that they need to algebraically rewrite

$\sqrt{(n+1)} - \sqrt{n} = e$ so that n is given in terms of e. It is not surprising that the group fails to do this, given that it is a substantially more difficult equation to solve than the previous one with which they had some difficulties. Mu starts out confidently, with the hypothesis that if both sides of the equation are squared then all the square root signs will conveniently disappear:

[Extract 7.5, tape 2, side A, lines 506-510]

Mu: I don't think that will be a problem will it.
Delta: No. That's right isn't it. We can factorise that.
Mu: We can take the square of it and get rid of every square root right? For any n.
Delta: No, you can have it as um … square root in that place … bracket …

However, when Mu applies the hypothesis to the equation he notices something unusual:[5]

[Extract 7.5, tape 2, side A, lines 514-516]

Mu: This is a dodgy one, this is. 'Cause like if you square it …
Delta: … you still get done with two n's.
Mu: You're going to get 1 equals epsilon, aren't you? Like n minus … n.

In the conversation that follows we see members of the group providing a number of different interpretations and suggestions in trying to deal with Mu's conclusion derived in extract 7.5. Delta offers the first suggestion which is that Mu's conclusion is a global counterexample to the original conjecture that the limit of $\sqrt{(n+1)} - \sqrt{n}$ is 0, as the following extract shows:

[Extract 7.6, tape 2, side A, lines 526-528]

Delta: That would mean … there's no limit. No value for epsilon, for N, sorry.
Kappa: Yeah.
(long pause)

After Kappa voices support the group falls silent for a considerable time. They are obviously not happy with the way their work has turned out. They also refuse to accept that their initial conjecture has been refuted by Mu's conclusion, relying on their intuition, or possibly the authority of the previous week's plenary session, that

---

5 Mu's reasoning is as follows:
   $\sqrt{(N+1)} - \sqrt{N} = e$
   $(\sqrt{(N+1)} - \sqrt{N})^2 = e^2$
   $N + 1 - N = e^2$ (this is the false step)
   Therefore $1 = e^2$ which implies $1 = e$

the limit must be 0. This results in the group trying out several different strategies in order to evaluate $\sqrt{(n+1)} - \sqrt{n} = e$ and obtain a sensible answer or to try and interpret the strange answer their previous evaluations have given them in order to make sense of them, as is shown in the extracts that follow.

The first proposal, by Delta, is to rewrite the equation using a different form of notation, in the hope that the same conclusion is not reached:

[Extract 7.7, tape 2, side A, lines 548-554]

Delta: Couldn't you combine them?
Kappa: Combine them.
Delta: Well, we have it written down like n plus one to the half minus n to the half ... there's no way of making them ... combining them is there?
Phi: What, you mean like n plus 1 minus n to the half?
Delta: Yeah, something like that, yeah.
Mu: You're left without an n again.

Unsurprisingly a new notation does not result in a new result, given that the group has made the same mistake as outlined in footnote 5. Once again the group members focus on the strange result, and try again to interpret it. This time Delta recalls that they are not specifically dealing with an equality, but an inequality instead. With this in mind he asks the following questions:

[Extract 7.8, tape 2, side A, lines 563-569]

Delta: 1 is greater than epsilon. Apparently 1 is greater than epsilon. What's that supposed to say?
(pause)
Delta: 1 is greater than all the counting numbers or something?
Mu: That's stupid, isn't it. That's awful. (unclear) You can have any number is greater than 1.
(laughter)

Delta's questions in the above extract are an attempt to interpret the strange result the group have derived. Mu's rewording of Delta's interpretation causes everyone in the group to laugh, which I would suggest signifies that they recognise that the result obtained makes no sense. Kappa sums up the groups feelings in line 575 at this point, when he exclaims, "I think we've got stuck!" However, a short while later Delta has another idea, and puts forward a second proposal for evaluating the equation:

[Extract 7.9, tape 2, side A, lines 584-590]

Delta: Can you do it with logs?
Phi: Oh, right.
Delta: With the power? Put it to the power and use logs.
Mu: You can try it.
Kappa: Yeah.
Mu: You've got nothing to lose so ...
Kappa: Yeah.

However even this approach fails to lead to a solution[6]. In an anticlimactic finish the group fails to solve the equation before the tape is stopped.

The use of the formal definition of a limit provides an interesting case study for the investigation. The students are already convinced that they know the limits of the sequences they are working with, having verified them both intuitively and through the authority of a classroom plenary session. Yet the worksheet requires them to test the accuracy of their initial convictions in a formal manner. I would conjecture that for most students such a formal verification would provide less conviction than their intuition does.

Despite the abstract content of the material, and the difficulties caused by this to the students, their work shows many of the elements identified by Lakatos as part of the proving process. We have seen members of the group through discussion identify steps breaking down a conjecture, steps that can be identified as the constituents of a proof-analysis. We have seen the group put forward counterexamples and then devise methods for dealing with them. In the two cases examined above it is the group members' algebraic skills which are letting them down, rather than any intrinsic difficulties with proving. However, it is still not clear from the analyses whether the group realises they are engaged in proof-like activities, or even if they fully appreciate what they are doing.

---

6 For completeness, here is a solution obtained by one of the other groups:
$\sqrt{(N+1)} - \sqrt{N} = e$ [eqn 1]
$(\sqrt{(N+1)} - \sqrt{N})(\sqrt{(N+1)} + \sqrt{N}) = e(\sqrt{(N+1)} + \sqrt{N})$
$N + 1 - N = e(\sqrt{(N+1)} + \sqrt{N})$
Therefore $\sqrt{(N+1)} + \sqrt{N} = 1/e$ [eqn 2]
eqn 2 - eqn 1 gives $(1/e) - e = 2\sqrt{N}$ from which N can easily be found in terms of e.

7.4 *An algebraic approach to series*

In the last half hour the group starts working on an algebraic approach to the summing of geometric series. When trying to find the sum of 1/3 + 1/9 + 1/27 ... after having worked through an algebraic method of summation[7] a misunderstanding causes the group to conclude that the answer is 2/3. Although this mistake is perpetuated through the whole of the conversation that follows, and the general level of mathematical sophistication shown by the group is low, it is interesting that many elements of proof-like knowledge are still present in their discussions. Members of the group continue to present generalisations and conjectures and counterexamples, and at one point Phi convinces the group that one of his conjectures is correct through an utterance that can be classified as a thought experiment which admits a proof-analysis. It is intriguing that, despite failing to produce anything that a mathematician would consider to have mathematical merit, the group's conversation mirrors many of the elements identified by Lakatos as constituting the process of mathematical discovery that I reviewed in chapter 5.

7.4.1 *The origin of a conjecture*

The initial error appears to occur when the group tries to work through the method presented in worksheet 3. I have been unable to determine with certainty why this error occurs, although it appears to be due to a combination of factors such as members of the group talking across each other, mishearing each other, and drawing conclusions from each others statements out of context, combined with an initial mis-evaluation of the final equation of the algebraic approach by Phi:

> [Extract 8.1: tape 3, side A, lines 274-284]
>
> Phi: If you, if it, if this is a third of the whole sequence, right?[8]
> Delta: Yeah.
> Phi: Eventually the sequence is gonna converge very close to 1.[9]

---

7 The algebraic approach as described in worksheet 3 is reproduced here:
   let S = 1/3 + 1/9 + 1/27 + ...
   then (1/3)S = 1/9 + 1/27 + ...
   so S - (1/3)S = 1/3, from which S can be found
8 Phi is referring to line 2 of the algebraic approach.
9 I do not know why Phi comes to this conclusion.

Delta: Yeah.
Phi: So 1/3 of the whole sequence is then gonna be 2/3.
Delta: 2/3.
Phi: It's gonna ...
Delta: Yeah.
Phi: ..., you gonna be left with nearly 2/3 (unclear) the third.
Delta: Yeah, so that's more how you can sort out cause that converges to what was it, 1, that converges towards 2/3, hm, isn't it.

This marks the first occasion of the error. A few lines further on Mu queries the answer of 2/3. Unfortunately his alternative to Phi and Delta's answer, which is that the sum of the sequence is 1/3, is even more blatantly incorrect. This introduces an interesting social phenomenon — an obviously false conjecture can add credence to a more subtly false conjecture postulated at the same time. Kappa, assisted by Delta and Phi, quickly silences Mu with an explanation supporting Phi's conjecture whose reasoning I do not understand:

[Extract 8.2: tape 3, side A, lines 293-304]

Mu: Why does that converge to 2/3? That. Why does that con...
Delta: Yeah.
Mu: ...verge? Shouldn't that be 1/3?
Kappa: Yeah, it should be 2/3 because, because ...
Phi: Right, I think it ...
Delta: Yep, and you ...
Kappa: ... because you got a 1/3 there, and it's a 1/3+2/3 = 1.
Delta: ... and you times it, by a multiple 1/3.
Phi: I think you ... you've had one out, and we've had it converging to 1 as well, haven't we?
Delta: Yeah, yeah.
Phi: In my head. Yes. Much.

Throughout this part of the conversation the students are repeatedly interrupting each other and trying to pre-empt each other. This could be the reason why suspect conclusions and arguments are not queried.

After a brief re-examination of the series 1/2 + 1/4 + 1/8 ... the group proceeds to examine the sum of the series 1/3 + 1/9 + 1/27 ... using a calculator. The following conversation occurs:

[Extract 8.3: tape 3, side A, lines 314-331]

Delta: Right, got it. A third plus what's next?
Phi: 1/9.
Kappa: 1/9.

Delta: Next one?
Phi: 1/27.
Kappa: 1/27. Um.
Delta: Just say that'll do.
Kappa: Which is?
Delta: Wicked!
Mu: Sure that's right?
Kappa: Yeah, that's it, that's going towards 1, isn't it?
(pause)
Delta: Is it one over (inaudible muttering).
(pause)
Delta: That's converging towards a third.
Mu: No it's not.
Delta: No it's not, it's going higher isn't it?
Kappa: Towards 1/2.

Empirically they have come up with the correct answer. Kappa states it clearly in his last utterance in extract 8.3 — "Towards 1/2". However, Phi is not willing to relinquish his original conjecture that the sum of the series is 2/3, as the continuation of the above extract shows:

[Extract 8.4: tape 3, side A, lines 332-341]

Phi: Towards 1/2!
Delta: Well, what's the next figure then?
Phi: It's going to take a bloody long time to get up to 2/3 isn't it?
Mu: You sure it's 1/2 for 3, yeah?
Kappa: Yeah.
Mu: OK, what's next?
Delta: Where's 243 come from?
Kappa: It's 3, innit?
Delta: 243 comes from?
Kappa: It's such a small figure it's not going to be worth worrying about is it?

A lot is happening in the conversation. The group's cohesion appears to be fragmenting as Kappa and Mu engage in a discussion about why the series sums to 1/2, whilst Phi's assertion that the series sums to 2/3 appears to be ignored. However, the next sentence in the conversation draws the group back together when Phi, by generalising from his incorrect answer puts forward a bold "naïve conjecture" regarding the sum of any series:

[Extract 8.5: tape 3, side A, lines 342-356]

Phi: Well. I think you double the original figure. Like a half will always be equal to 1. And the your 1/3 will be equal to 2/3. That's what that means, isn't it?
Kappa: No, it looks like it's converging to 1/2.
Mu: But how come 1/2?

Phi: It can't converge to 1/2.
Delta: It can con...
Phi: You're on a half there, aren't you? You're coming up to 1/243, 1 over...
Kappa: Yeah, I mean the numbers are so small, the numbers are getting smaller and smaller.
Phi: It's the second term ...
Kappa: And smaller.
Phi: ..., that there makes sense to say that the sequence goes, converges to 2/3, doesn't it?
Kappa: Yep?
Delta: Yeah.

Phi's belief that the sequence sums to 2/3 is based on the conjecture that the sum of a sequence is "double the original figure". This immediately refuted by Kappa, but Phi responds by disagreeing with Kappa and providing a false counterexample. He claims that the empirical sum has already reached 1/2 in line 348. Mu's question, "But how come 1/2" is interesting, and it is a shame that the group does not consider it. Unfortunately Mu is the weakest member of the group, often speaking quietly, and he is edged out of the conversation by the louder, more forceful Phi. Despite the fact that Phi's assertion, "You're on a half there, aren't you", is incorrect, no one picks up on this. Kappa repeats his statement about the decreasing significance of later terms, previously made at the end of extract 8.4 in support of the series summing to a half, but is once again overruled by Phi, whose explains that his answer "makes sense". Phi is now convinced of truth of his conjecture, and has gained the support of Delta. This conjecture is held by the group for the duration of the lesson, subject to minor modification. The reasons for this are examined in the next section.

7.4.2 The development of a proof

An indication of the fact that increased familiarity with the basics of the topic is leading to an increased reliance on proof-like methods is to be found in the verbalisation of a thought experiment by Phi. Unfortunately the experiment is false, although as will be shown later, it is sufficiently convincing to the rest of the group for them to adopt it as a justification for Phi's conjecture that the total sum of a positive series is equal to twice the initial term of the series:

[Extract 9.1: tape 3, side A, lines 357-370]

Phi: Yeah? So if you put, leave 1/3 over there then you got 2/3. I mean with 1/2 we were doing it according to (unclear). I mean you're starting off with 1/2 and then you're chopping it up into little bits. So you gonna have another 1/2. If you start off with 1/3, the you've got another 1/3 that you're chopping up into tiny little bits. So it's gonna, be 2/3 isn't it? You're never going to get more than 2/3. We, we always had just 1, over there. If you started off with, started off with, what, 1/4 it would never be more than 2/4. Yeah? No, but each time you're chopping it up and chopping it up and then, you're never, whatever your original thing is, yeah, you're never going to converge to more than where you are, cause you're taking, you're taking that and then you're chopping it up in half, and you keep chopping that in half and then each time you get, you get, and it's never gonna be more than that 1/2 that's, that's what I mean.

Kappa: Yeah. That's right. It goes to 2/3.

Phi: So basically the whole thing will converge up to 2/3.

Although Phi is having difficulties explaining himself to the rest of the group, and often falls back on specific examples to illustrate his argument, the above excerpt suggests that he has a particular thought experiment in mind. We can make sense of it in Lakatosian terms as follows. The thought experiment which Phi is describing relies on a central idea of "chopping up fractions" (line 364) repeatedly *ad infinitum*. The following proof-analysis breaks this idea down somewhat more elegantly that Phi's halting explanation. It should be noted that the list of lemmas, have been cast in a form which I have specifically chosen. The reason for this is that I believe the proof-analysis I present is a reasonable interpretation of Phi's utterances, although I recognise that it is not the only interpretation that could be made. However, I consider writing out Phi's argument in the following form helps to clarify his conversation and possibly the thought processes behind it. I have also presented a paragraph providing more information on each lemma after it is stated, including an indication of where I have drawn my interpretation from.

1. The series $S_1 = 1/2 + 1/4 + 1/8 \ldots$ and $S_2 = 1/3 + 1/9 + 1/27 +\ldots$ are analogous, in that a method that provides the correct answer for S_1 must provide the correct answer for S_2.

This lemma is not explicitly presented by Phi. However, he does begin his monologue by referring to a sequence starting with 1/3, and then switches to talking about a sequence starting with 1/2 having the same properties, and finally, draws in another example starting with a 1/4. This strongly suggests to me that Phi senses an analogy, or commonality, between the examples. Unfortunately this lemma is false.

2. By using the method of "chopping in half" we get $1/2 = 1/4 + 1/4$, and then by "chopping in half" one of the $1/4$'s we get $1/2 = 1/4 + 1/8 + 1/8$ and so on repeatedly which shows that $1/2$ is converged to by $1/4 + 1/8 + 1/16$ ...

Phi is referring to this lemma, and the process behind it, when he talks about "starting off with $1/2$ and then you're chopping it into little bits". In this instance, Phi's reasoning is sound. However, he reveals a certain lack of understanding in his transferral of this lemma to other similar series, for example in the latter part of his monologue when he repeats the phrase "you're chopping it up" in reference to the series S_2. This is discussed in further detail later on.

3. By using lemma 2) and substituting we find that S_1 converges to $1/2 + 1/2$.

I have included this lemma as a clarifying step in the reasoning behind Phi's thought experiment. Phi, however, bundles this lemma up with the previous one and the next one in his explanation.

4. By using lemma 3) we see that S_1 is converging to twice the first term of the series, or $2 * 1/2$, which equals 1.

Again, see lemma 3).

5. Using lemma 1) and lemma 4) we can see that S_2 converges to $2*1/3$, or $2/3$[10].

The final step is the application of the analogy assumed in lemma 1) to lemma 4).

Thus Phi's explanation has been broken down into its constituent parts and presented as a proof-analysis in support of the conjecture that S_2 sums to $2/3$. That Phi has this proof-analysis in mind is confirmed by a later discussion with Delta and Mu:

[Extract 9.2: tape 3, side A, lines 407-418]

Delta: That one'll go up to 2/3?
Kappa: Yeah.
Phi: That one'll always, whatever your original one is, right, that's a third, this is a half.

---

10 This is of course wrong, as S_2 actually equals $1/2$.

Delta: And that one.
Phi: Yeah. And whatever that is, yeah, you can't, I mean, you can't, to get 1, you're going to have to have 3 of those 1/3, and your never going to have 3 1/3s because we're only starting off with a 1/3, and then it's getting smaller and smaller denominations of the next 1/3. So whatever that first figure is, it's going to cut down from there.
Mu: Oh, with all the other bits adding up to 1/3! Isn't it?
Phi: I mean, basically, yeah. It's gonna add up to whatever that original is.[11]

Mu has interpreted Phi's explanation in the same manner as I have above (for example, when Mu exclaims, "Oh, with all the other bits adding up to 1/3!"), and Phi agrees with Mu's interpretation.

Returning to the point at which Phi presents his thought experiment (extract 9.1), we find that although Kappa is convinced by Phi's explanation, Mu has some doubts. Remembering the group's previous empirical investigation into the sum of the series using a calculator (extract 8.3) which resulted in S_2 appearing to sum to 1/2, he presents Phi with a global counter-example. The conversation proceeds as follows:

[Extract 9.3: tape 3, side A, lines 372-378]

Mu: So why does that converge to a half then?
Phi: It doesn't.
Delta: It doesn't because you're just not going far enough.
Phi: Because you're just not going far enough. It will go up to 2/3. Which isn't that far off there, I mean that's ... but you won't get more than that. Seriously, that's it isn't it if that's your 1/3.
Mu: Yeah.

Phi and Delta overcome Mu's reminder of the previously discovered counterexample by claiming that provided enough terms are added up the series will exceed 1/2 and head for 2/3. By doing this they are denying that Mu's counterexample is really a counterexample at all. Mu, who is by no means the strongest member of the group, concurs. Although their mathematical reasoning is faulty, the group is following the Lakatosian pattern of proofs and refutations, as was outlined in chapter 5. It should also be noted that mathematical reasoning has over-ruled empirical evidence in this instance.

Despite the fact that the group is now convinced that Phi's

---

11 Like Mu, I assume that "the original" means the first term of the series, and that "It's" refers to the sum of the rest of the terms. Phi uses the term "the original" in several other places to mean the first term of the series.

reasoning is sound, they proceed to elaborate the proof with a diagram:

[Extract 9.4: tape 3, side A, lines 389-402]

Phi: Well, go back on this one. If you start off with 1/3s.
Delta: Well, yeah you, I mean, you could do it, you mean, like that.
Phi: Yeah.
Delta: Just a circle. Right. You got the thirds, there.
Kappa: Yeah.
Delta: So every time you third it (unclear). Then you've got 1/9, adding a twenty, adding ...
Phi: 1/27, yeah.
Delta: A 1/9. Just leave that there.
Phi: Yeah.
Mu: That's all going to add up to 2/3, isn't it?
Phi: Basically, yeah.
Kappa: Yeah.
Delta: Yeah.

Unfortunately I do not have a copy of the group's rough work during the session. I believe that figure 7.1 below, which may contain a circle similar to the one drawn by the group, can however be used to clarify why Phi's proof is incorrect and how to correct it:

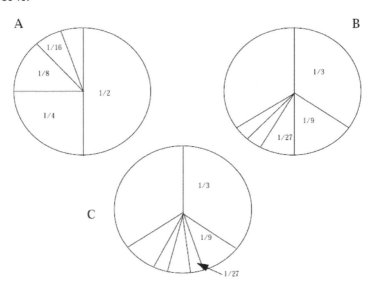

Figure 7.1 Circles used to represent sums

Circle A shows visually why the series $S_1 = 1/2 + 1/4 + 1/8$ ...

sums to 1. In circle B the segments have been labelled incorrectly, but if this error is not noticed the circle shows why it might be credible that $S_2 = 1/3 + 1/9 + 1/27 \ldots$ sums to 2/3. Finally, circle C shows how Phi's proof could be adjusted to demonstrate that S_2 actually sums to 1/2.

Phi has overlooked that "chopping up" fractions in the case of S_1 involves successive halving, whereas "chopping up" in the case of S_2 involves thirding. Therefore the guilty lemma in the proof-analysis is lemma 1, in that the series are not as analogous as Phi thought. This can be considered an error of generalisation and specialization, as the "rule" generalised from S_1 does not specialise correctly in the case of S_2. However, the underlying reasoning of the thought experiment is sound.

7.5 Summary

In this chapter, transcriptions of the work of a group of students were analysed chronologically in the light of the theory developed in the preceding chapters, to empirically ground that theory and to test its usefulness as a perspective on students' notions of proof. In this section I provide a summary of the analysis and relate it to specific parts of the theory of proof.

7.5.1 The origination of conjectures

A common thread that ran through the work of the students was the constant process of conjecturing, corroboration and refutation at various levels. However, it was in the first third of the analysis that most of the conjecturing and refutation could be seen to occur, setting the foundation for later proof-like activity. Although no conjectures were obtained through deductive guessing, a variety of naïve guessing strategies were utilised by members of the group to generate conjectures.

The most common strategy for generating conjectures consisted of a limited form of induction, whereby members of the group proposed formulae on the basis of a quick inspection of the sequences, followed by empirical testing to corroborate or refute the conjecture. In the process of refining some of the formulae members of the group evidenced forms of naïve conjecturing through generalising and specialisation, particularly in the case of determining the starting points of sequences. Finally, naïve conjecture through analogy by transferring knowledge about one question to a similar question was also observed. With regard to the origination phase of conjectures, my review and adaptation of the work of Dawson (1969), Polya (1986) and Lakatos (1976) in chapter 5 appears to provide a sound basis for the analysis and description of the group's activities.

7.5.2 *Student proof-like activity*

In the middle third of the analysis the group developed a proof-analysis for proving what the limit of a sequence was, although the underlying thought experiment was not explicitly revealed. The proof-analysis was then applied to a second sequence, with only the group's lack of algebraic skill preventing them from completing their work. Naturally during this process the group were still proposing and testing conjectures. However, there was a significant difference between this part of the group's work and previous conjecturing. Some of the conjecturing concerned breaking down an initial conjecture into sub-conjectures, or lemmas, thus constructing a proof-analysis for the initial conjecture.

In constructing their first proof-analysis the group did not develop their own thought experiment on which the decomposition of their initial conjecture was to be based. Rather, the thought experiment was provided for them in the form of the formal definition of a limit. On the one hand this could be seen as a loose interpretation of a thought experiment, particularly given that the group starts out not fully understanding the definition. On the other hand adopting the formal definition as the thought experiment basis of a proof could be interpreted as the group picking up an historical mathematical tradition. Furthermore, in the process of developing their proof-analysis, the group came to understand the definition more fully — an example of a proof-analysis pointing more clearly towards a thought experiment.

In the final third of the analysis one member of the group, Phi, came up with a significant thought experiment on which to base a proof of the sum of a series. Unfortunately an error in the resulting break-down of the thought experiment into a proof-analysis of sub-lemmas resulted in the group accepting an empirically falsified conjecture as a theorem. However, this case clearly illustrated that although the group failed to construct what a professional mathematician would recognise as a valid proof, the underlying reasoning and the pattern of working exhibited by the group were sound when interpreted in the light of the theory. Furthermore, it revealed an instance where the students were more convinced by deductive argument than by an empirical refutation. In the final analysis, the adoption of Lakatos' (1976) hitherto overlooked approach to proof as thought experiment coupled with proof-analysis provided an insightful way to examine the group's proof-like activities.

8 Conclusions and implications

8.1 Introduction

The purpose of this, the final chapter of the study, is to present a conclusion and a summary of the work conducted. It is also to outline the implications for further research and to review the limitations of the study. Recall that at the start of this work four questions were raised. The first two questions were: what are students' current notions of the nature and role of mathematical proof, and how do students develop notions of proof? These questions arose, and were partially answered, in two published pilot studies (Finlow-Bates, 1994, p.344-351, Finlow-Bates *et al.*, 1993, p.252-259). As I argued in chapter 1, a fuller discussion of these two questions required the consideration of two more: what is the nature of mathematical proof, and what does to engage in the activity of proving mean? How and to what extent these questions have been addressed is the topic of the following four sections.

8.2 Summary

The study consists of two sections. In the first part the question of what constitutes mathematical proof was discussed. I pursued in depth a hitherto overlooked approach to proof drawn from Lakatos' (1976) *Proofs and Refutations*; in which proof was identified as thought experiment coupled with proof-analysis in order to break down conjectures into sub-conjectures and lemmas. The purpose of this decomposition was to afford criticism of the conjecture a wider target, thus increasing the opportunities for discovering counter-examples or refutations. The underlying philosophical perspective of the study is therefore in one sense a critical fallibilistic one.

However, such a philosophy, although supplying a number of insights into the nature and purpose of proof within mathematics, cannot fully explain all the attributes and expectations mathematicians associate with proof, nor the practices and traditions surrounding it. As a result I discussed social theories of mathematical knowledge, in order to provide the theory of proof with a deeper grounding. In this discussion Platonistic theories which regard mathematical knowledge as being external to the learner and eternal and true in nature were discarded in favour of a more socially and culturally focused theory, based on the ideas of, amongst others, Wittgenstein, Rotman and Restivo. Although fallibilist and social theories of knowledge do not necessarily belong together they do complement each other, and it was my belief that they would provide a fruitful avenue for research. A further reason for adopting a relativist rather than a realist approach to the nature of knowledge lies with the fact that realist theories of knowledge have for a considerable time been the traditional implicit theories underlying much academic research. Ironically the tacit and traditional acceptance of Platonistic foundations for mathematics provides further support for social theories of knowledge.

The second part of the study presented the design and implementation of an investigation of students' notions of proof within a first year mathematics classroom in South Bank University. The theory constructed in the first section was taken as a theoretical underpinning for this investigation. A group of four students in the classroom working on questions concerning the topic of sequences and series were audio taped and the recordings were transcribed and analysed. One can identify two extremes in the possible methodological foundations for investigations within this area of mathematics education. One is the verification of a scientific hypothesis through large scale statistical experiments. Such an approach is unsuitable for an investigation concerned with potentially unquantifiable concepts such as understanding, insight and intuition, all of which are considered in this study. The other extreme consists of the generation of a grounded theory from a qualitative study. Once again, such a radical approach is unsuitable, as the topic of mathematical proof has been subject to continuing interest and inquiry within the field of mathematics education, with works such as Lakatos' (1976) *Proofs and Refutations*, Davis and Hersh's (1981) *the Mathematical Experience* and Hanna's (1983) *Rigorous Proof in Mathematics Education* providing new perspectives on proof and its role in teaching. Given such a plethora of material on proof I argued that a theory driven investigation was most suitable, but due to the nature of the topic such an investigation should be qualitative in nature. The aim of the second part of the study can therefore best be seen as one of grounding the theoretically constructed perspective of the nature of proof.

8.3 *Conclusions*

In this section I examine the conclusions which were drawn in the various chapters of the book. These conclusions can be split into three rough categories: conclusions drawn from the initial studies reviewed in chapter 2, "A review of the preliminary research" which had a significant influence on the overall direction taken in this study; conclusions arising from the theoretical developments of the study; and finally, conclusions drawn by examining relation of the final empirical investigation to the theory of proof.

In chapter 2 I reviewed two preliminary studies which were conducted in order to provide a starting point for the examination of students' notions of proof. They had a marked influence on the main study, both in the construction of a theory of proof and in the design and execution of the final investigation. From a theoretical point of view it was revealed that an underlying theory of proof was highly desirable for conducting an empirical investigation. In relation to the final investigation the main influence of the preliminary studies was the decision to adopt a qualitative approach to the gathering and interpretation of experimental data, which entailed the design of a qualitative research methodology, as outlined in chapter 6. A final conclusion, arising primarily from the results of the second study, was the decision to approach proof as a process rather than a learning outcome. This set the foundations for the adoption of a fallibilist approach to proof.

In chapter 3 and chapter 4 I discussed previous work in the areas of mathematics education and proof. The first half of the review examined notions connected with proof, such as justification, explanation, convincing, generalisation, abstraction and intuition. I concluded that these notions could be best described as "aspects of mathematical proof": important features held in common by many proofs, but which individually fail to describe in any detail what actually constitutes a proof. The second part of the review covered a number of classification schemes that have been put forward to identify different types of proof according to, for example, their level of generality, sophistication, or formality. I decided that although significant results had been obtained through the use of such schemes, for the purposes of my study it would be more profitable to search for a different approach to the question of what constitutes proof.

This different approach was found in the work of Lakatos (1976), as detailed in chapter 5. Lakatos is well-known on two counts: his description of the growth of mathematical knowledge as occurring through the process of proofs and refutations, and his development of quasi-empiricism — a philosophy of mathematics based strongly on Popper's critical fallibilism. Although broadly taking on board the method of proofs and refutations and the tenets of quasi-empiricism, it is in the study of a third concept outlined by Lakatos that this study is at its most original. This concept is the characterisation of proof as a thought experiment coupled with a proof-analysis, as outlined in chapter 5 and the summary above. The relationship of these three Lakatosian notions of mathematics and proof to the empirical investigation presented in chapter 6 and chapter 7 are examined below.

Lakatos (1976) characterises the growth of mathematical knowledge through the development of proofs by a process of conjecture and refutation. The occurrence of a problem gives rise to a conjecture or guess put forward as a possible solution. The conjecture is then to be subjected to criticism with the intention of refuting it. There was ample evidence in the empirical investigation that the group of students did on many occasions follow the general pattern as outlined by Lakatos. Indeed, on occasions members of the group managed to put forward and then refute flurries of conjectures, and it was a heartening fact that this process usually resulted in an improved answer. This observed behaviour justifies the selection of Lakatos' quasi-empiricism and the method of proofs and refutations as a philosophical basis for the construction of a theory of proof.

The theory proved fruitful in describing how the group constructed proofs; notably on two occasions. On the first occasion the group was attempting to prove a conjecture that they had arrived at, hypothesising that the limit of a sequence was 1. It was possible to determine from the transcripts that they managed to break the original conjecture down into a number of lemmas, failing to produce a suitable proof only due to a lack of algebraic skills required to successfully generate a final lemma. Thus essentially the group produced a proof-analysis, although the thought experiment which it pointed to was somewhat obscured by its reliance on the formal definition of a limit.

On the second occasion Phi managed to produce a clear description of a thought experiment designed to prove a later conjecture concerning the sum of a series. Unfortunately the conjecture was flawed, but the thought experiment - based upon the idea of "chopping in half" the conjectured answer repeatedly - successfully convinced the other members of the group to accept the conjecture as proven, in the face of contrary empirical evidence.

Therefore a final conclusion is that the investigation revealed the students to be capable of constructing arguments with a proof-like structure, even though the semantic content of the arguments was often flawed. The characterisation of a proof as a thought experiment coupled with a proof-analysis therefore constituted a fruitful approach to the notion of proof. It prompts me to suggest that a strategy that might be successful in developing students notions of proof would be to take a reflective approach to work conducted in the classroom. If at the end of each work session the students presented parts of their work they believed to contain elements of proving, then with appropriate teacher intervention which draws attention to the proof-like nature of their work in a interspective and retrospective manner (Mason, 1994), the students might be more successful in developing notions of proof. This strategy would have two advantages. Firstly, the students would be presented with "success-stories" within the context of their own classroom on which to build, rather than dry examples from textbooks or the teacher's own experience. Secondly, the opportunity for the class to engage in a proof-and-refutations discussion would naturally arise.

8.4 Limitations

The level to which the conclusions of this study can be generalised is limited by the choice of philosophical basis for an investigation into the nature of, and students' understanding of, mathematical proof. Due to the selection of a Lakatosian approach to mathematics and the role which it ascribes to proof within mathematics a bias is introduced into the study; in the sense that any philosophical basis requires the subject to be viewed from a particular perspective. Furthermore, it cannot even be claimed that the exposition of Lakatos' work and its interpretation within the light of a social theory of mathematics is the only possible one, as it depends on the writer's interpretation and integration of these standpoints. However, as was justified in the introduction of chapter 5, these limitations were necessary. Secondly, to ascribe any level of absolute truth or generalisability to this work, relying as it does on fallibilism, would be by its very nature a contradiction. Rather, the criteria for the study have been those of internal consistency and the search for interesting and fruitful lines of research within mathematics education and the academic tradition.

The investigation focused on the definition of proof as a thought experiment coupled with a proof-analysis, and examined the work of the students from a quasi-empirical perspective. However, another part of the theory of proof, namely the part concerned with mathematical knowledge as being social in nature, was not examined. Two reasons were given in chapter 6, "Methodology and design of the investigation", for this: conducting a local study of the social nature of mathematical knowledge would remove the investigation from its natural setting, contravening one of the accepted principles for qualitative research, and more importantly, by widening the scope of the study to attempt to include an empirical examination of the social nature of mathematical knowledge would detract from the focal point of the study, namely investigating students' notions of proof.

A further limitation that must be noted is that this study is not aimed at presenting a new instructional model for the teaching of proof. Decisions as to the teaching of any area of mathematics rely on a broader base including amongst other elements psychological issues such as theories of learning the nature of the learners, sociological issues such as the nature of the community in which the teaching is to occur, whether it be a university or a school, and even political issues such as legal requirements for the curriculum and the structure and policies of the educational institution. Despite this I have tentatively put forward some suggestions in the conclusions section of this chapter with regard to teaching strategies that I consider to have merit in the teaching of proof.

8.5 *Implications for further research*

To maintain the cohesiveness of a report and remain within the time limits imposed upon research by external factors it is almost always necessary to narrow the scope of a study beyond what was initially expected. Such was also the case with this work. Within the main body of the book I have tried to indicate the areas where work was curtailed due to these factors. This, the final section of the book, provides an overview of these areas and addresses other areas suitable for further research.

The theoretical basis on which the study rests was constructed from primarily a philosophical approach. Adopting a stance with a more psychological slant with regards to how students learn could lead to a more encompassing theoretical base, with more scope for the design of classroom activities. Which epistemology to select from the numerous orientations available would have to be at the discretion of the researcher.

The question of intentionality within the group of students with regard to proving could benefit from further investigation, both theoretical and empirical. It is not clear from the investigation how aware the students are of their engagement with proof. It is possible they do not have the correct terminology to describe what they are doing (see Finlow-Bates, 1994 for an example of this), or that they do not connect words such as "proof" with their activities. They may not even be consciously aware of what they have achieved. From a theoretical point of view it appears that the question of what it means to be conscious of proving needs further investigation, especially as awareness and reflection are often considered to be important issues within the mathematics education community. A final point is that the intent of students involved with proof is necessarily different to that of practising mathematicians. For example, for the practising mathematician the generation of new mathematics is of great importance; something which is seen to have little, if any, importance by students who are usually more concerned with passing exams. Given the importance attributed to proof in the creation of new mathematics, this point must have a significant bearing on the question of awareness of proving.

Linked to the students' awareness of their engagement with proof is the issue of clarification of terms used in the development of proofs and arguments. In *Proofs and Refutations* Lakatos charts the clarification of ambiguities of referents, that is, the links between referring nouns and the ideas to which they point are strengthened through explication in the process of improving through proving. For example, the core idea of a "polyhedron" is expanded significantly during the examination of the Euler conjecture. It can be argued that there is a sense of confluence between this and getting students to clarify their use of indefinite pronouns and even nouns (Mason, personal communication). The examination and development of this conjecture could provide a fruitful extension of the Lakatosian theory of proof presented in this investigation.

The classroom investigation was of an observational nature. Teaching materials were designed for the course without the investigation in mind, and the teaching, and in particular the teacher interventions, occurred as the lecturers saw fit and not according to any scheme proposed by the research. An interesting area for further research would be to conduct a full teaching experiment rather than an investigation, along the lines of, say, Steffe's (1991) social constructivist teaching experiments into children's counting schemes (see also Carpenter, 1985), with teacher/student interactions being planned in order to test continually elements of the theory during the experiment. Such an experiment would however require a further development in the underlying theory of proof along more psychological lines, as described in the previous paragraph.

Brodie (1994) has dealt with questions of social pressure within the workings of a group in the mathematics classroom by focusing in particular on how notions of "ownership" of mathematical knowledge affect group interactions and the development of further knowledge. It was observed in my investigation that the group used techniques other than those identified by Lakatos (1976) in dealing with counter-examples, for example the technique of counter-example ignoring. A potentially fruitful extension of the investigation could therefore consist of an examination of how social pressure within the group affected the development of proof-like knowledge, and to what extent Brodie's work on "ownership" could be applied to the "ownership" of proofs or refutations.

Finally, the theoretical basis proved to be useful for the interpretation of student activities within the context of a specific first year university mathematics classroom. It would be interesting to conduct similar investigations at different educational levels, for example in a secondary school classroom. In particular, the point at which students' arguments start to exhibit the structure of mathematical proof would seem worthy of attention.

9 References

Balacheff, N. (1987); Processus de preuve et situations de validation, in Educational Studies in Mathematics 18, p.147-176, D. Reidel Publishing Company: Dordrecht, the Netherlands.

Balacheff, N. (1988); Aspects of proof in pupil's practice of school mathematics, in Pimm, D. (ed); Mathematics, Teachers and Children, Hodder and Staughton: London, UK.

Balacheff, N. (1991); The benefits and limits of social interaction: the case of mathematical proof, in Bishop, A., Mellin-Olsen, S. and van Dormolen, J. (Eds.) (1991); Mathematical Knowledge: Its Growth through Teaching, Kluwer Academic Publishers: Dordrecht, the Netherlands.

Barbin, E. (1992); The Epistemological Roots of a Constructivist Interpretation of Teaching Mathematics, ICME-7, Curtin: Quebec, Canada.

Barnard, T. (1989); Is the proof in the practice? in Mathematics in School 9, p.9-13.

Barnes, D. and Todd, F. (1977); Communication and Learning in Small Groups, Routledge and Kegan Paul: London, UK.

Beaulieu, L. (1990); Proofs in expository writing - some examples from Bourbaki's early drafts, in Interchange 21 1, p.35-45, the Ontario Institute for Studies in Education: Ontario, Canada.

Bell, A. W. (1976); A study of pupils' proof-explanations in mathematical situations, in Educational Studies in Mathematics 7, p.23-40, D. Reidel Publishing Company: Dordrecht, the Netherlands.

Bell, A. W., Costello, J. and Küchermann, D. (1983); Research on Learning and Teaching, NFER-Nelson: Windsor, UK.

Berger, A. A. (1982); Semiological Analysis, in Media Analysis Techniques, p.14-43, Sage Publications: Beverly Hills, USA.

Bloor, D. (1983); Wittgenstein: A Social Theory of Knowledge, the Macmillan Press: London, UK.

Bloor, D. (1994); What can the sociologist of knowledge say about 2 + 2 = 4? in Ernest, P. (ed.); Mathematics, Education and Philosophy: an International Perspective, Burgess Science Press: Basingstoke, UK.

Blum, W. and Kirsh, A. (1991); Preformal proving: examples and reflections, in Educational Studies in Mathematics 22, p.183-203, Kluwer Academic Publishers: Dordrecht, the Netherlands.

Bogdan, R. C. and Biklen, S. K. (1992); Qualitative Research for Education: an Introduction to Theory and Methods, 2nd edition, Allyn Bacon: Boston, USA.

Brodie, K. (1994); Small Group Work and Ownership of Mathematical Knowledge, Unpublished M.Ed. thesis, University of Witwatersrand: Johannesburg, South Africa.

Bruner, J. S. (1979); Essays for the Left Hand, Harvard University Press: Cambridge, Massachusetts, USA.

Bruner, J. S. (1968), Towards a Theory of Instruction, Norton: New York, USA.

Burger, W. E. and Shaughnessy, J. M. (1986); Characterising the van Hiele levels of development in geometry, in Journal for Research in Mathematics Education 17, 1, p.31-48, NCTM: USA.

Chazan, D. (1993); High school geometry students justification for their views of empirical evidence and mathematical proof, in Educational Studies in Mathematics 24, p.359-387, Kluwer Academic Publishers: Dordrecht, the Netherlands.

Cobb, P. (1989); A double-edged sword, in the Journal for Research in Mathematics Education 20, 2, NCTM: Reston, Virginia, USA.

Cobb, P., Yackel, E. and Wood, T. (1992): Interaction and learning in mathematics classroom situations, Educational Studies in Mathematics 23, p.99-122, Kluwer Academic Press: Dordrecht, the Netherlands.

Coe, R. and Ruthven, K. (1994); Proof practices and constructs of advanced mathematics students, in the British Educational Research Journal 20, 1, p.41-53, Carfax Publishing Company: Oxford, UK.

Cohen, L. and Manion, L. (1994); Research Methods in Education

(4th edition), Routledge: New York, USA.

Davis, P. J. (1993); Visual theorems, in Educational Studies in Mathematics 24, p.333-344, Kluwer Academic Publishers: Dordrecht, the Netherlands.

Davis, P. J. and Hersh, R. (1981); The Mathematical Experience, Birkhauser: Boston, USA.

Dawson, A. J. (1969): The Implications of the Work of Popper, Polya, and Lakatos for a Model of Mathematics Instruction, unpublished Ph.D. thesis, Alberta, Canada.

de Villiers, M. (1990); The role and function of proof in mathematics, in Pythagoras 24, p.17-24, The Mathematical Association of Southern Africa: Centralhil, South Africa.

de Villiers, M. (1991); Pupils' needs for conviction and explanation within the context of geometry, in the Proceedings of the 15th International Conference on the Psychology of Mathematics Education , Vol 1, p.255-262, Italy.

Edwards, A. D. and Westgate, D. P. G. (1987); Investigating Classroom Talk, the Falmer Press: London, UK.

Edwards, J. A. and Lampert, M. D. (1993); Talking Data: Transcription and Coding in Discourse Research, Lawrence Erlbaum Associates: Hillsdale, USA.

Ernest, P. (1991); The Philosophy of Mathematics Education, Falmer Press: London, UK.

Ernest, P. (1994a); Constructing Mathematical Knowledge: Epistemology and Mathematical Education, Falmer Press: London, UK.

Ernest, P. (1994b); Mathematics, Education and Philosophy: an International Perspective, Burgess Science Press: Basingstoke, UK.

Ernest, P. (1995); The mythic quest of the hero: a semiotic analysis of mathematical proof, in the Proceedings of the 19th International Conference on the Psychology of Mathematics Education vol. 1, p.240, Recife, Brazil.

Fetterman, D. M. (1989); Ethnography: Step by Step, Sage Publications: Newbury Park, USA.

Finlow-Bates, K. (1994); First year mathematics students' notions of the role of informal proof and examples, in the Proceedings of the 18th International Conference on the Psychology of Mathematics Education Vol. 2, p.344-351, Lisbon, Portugal.

Finlow-Bates, K., Lerman, S. and Morgan, C. (1993); A survey of current concepts of proof held by first year mathematics students, in the Proceedings of the 17th International Conference on the Psychology of Mathematics Education Vol. 1, p.252-259, Tskuba, Japan.

Fischbein, E. (1982); Intuition and Proof, in For the Learning of Mathematics 3, 2, FLM Publishing Association: Montreal, Canada.

Fischbein, E. (1987); Intuition in Science and Mathematics; D. Reidel: Dordrecht, the Netherlands.

Fischbein, E., Tirosh, D. and Melamed, U. (1981); Is it possible to measure the intuitive acceptance of a mathematical statement?, in Educational Studies in Mathematics 12, p.491-512, D. Reidel Publishing Co.: Dordrecht, the Netherlands.

Furinghetti, F. and Paola, D. (1991); On Some Obstacles in Understanding Mathematical Texts, Proceedings of the 15th Conference of the International Group for the Psychology of Mathematics Education, Vol. II, p. 56-63, Italy.

Galbraith, P. L. (1981); Aspects of proving: A clinical investigation of process, in Educational Studies in Mathematics 12, p.1-28, D. Reidel Publishing Company: Dordrecht, the Netherlands.

Glaser, B. G. and Strauss, A. L. (1967); The Discovery of Grounded Theory; Strategies for Qualitative Research, Aldine Publishing Company: Chicago, USA.

Griffiths, H. B. (1971); Mathematical insight and mathematical curricula, in Educational Studies in Mathematics 4, p.153-165, D. Reidel Publishing Company: Dordrecht, the Netherlands.

Griffiths, H. B. (1978); Some comments on Macdonald's paper, in Educational Studies in Mathematics 9, p.421-427, D. Reidel Publishing Company: Dordrecht, the Netherlands.

Hanna, G. (1983); Rigorous Proof in Mathematics Education, OISE Press: Toronto, Canada.

Hanna, G. (1989); More than Formal Proof, For the Learning of Mathematics 9(1), p.20-23, FLM Publishing Association:

Montreal, Canada.

Hanna, G. (1990); Some pedagogical aspects of proof, in Interchange 21(1), p.6-13, the Ontario Institute for Studies in Education: Ontario, Canada.

Hanna, G. (1995); Challenges to the importance of proof, For the Learning of Mathematics 15(3), FLM Publishing Association: Vancouver, Canada.

Hanna, G. (1996); The ongoing value of proof, Proceedings of the 20th Conference of the International Group for the Psychology of Mathematics Education, Vol. I, p. 21-34, Valencia, Spain.

Harel, G. and Tall, D. (1991); The general, the abstract, and the generic in advanced mathematics; in For the Learning of Mathematics 11(1), p.38-42, FLM Publishing association: White Rock, Canada.

Harr, R. and Secord, P. F. (1972); The Explanation of Social Behaviour, Basil Blackwell: Oxford, UK.

Herrington, A. (1985); Writing in academic settings: a study of the contexts for writing in two college chemical engineering courses, in Research in the Teaching of English 19, 4, p.331-35.

Hersh, R. (1993); Proving is convincing and explaining, in Educational Studies in Mathematics 24, p.389-399, Kluwer Academic Publishers: Dordrecht, the Netherlands.

Hewitt, D. (1992); Train spotters' paradise, in Mathematics Teaching 140.

Hoffer, A. (1981); Geometry is more than proof, in Mathematics Teacher 74, p.11-18.

Horgan, J. (1993); The death of proof, in Scientific American, 269, 4, p.93-103.

Hospers, J. (1973); An Introduction to Philosophical Analysis, Unwin Brothers Ltd.: Old Woking, UK.

Jaworski, B. (1990); Is the proof in the practice: more than myths? in Mathematics in School 3, p.48-50.

Kaplan, A. (1989); Research methodology: Scientific methods, in Keeves, J. P. (ed); Educational Research, Methodology, and Measurement: An International Handbook, Pergammon Press:

New York, USA

Kieran, T. (1983); Axioms and intuition in mathematical knowledge building, in Proceedings of the 5th Conference of the North-American Chapter on the Psychology of Mathematics Education, p.67-73.

Kline, M. (1980); Mathematics - The Loss of Certainty, Oxford University Press: Oxford, UK.

Körner, S. (1962); The Philosophy of Mathematics, Harper and Row: New York, USA.

Kuhn, T. S. (1962); The Structure of Scientific Revolutions , the University of Chicago Press: Chicago, U.S.A.

Lakatos, I. (1976); Proofs and Refutations, Cambridge University Press: Cambridge, UK.

Lakatos, I. (1978); Mathematics, Science and Epistemology, Cambridge University Press: Cambridge.

Lakatos, I. (1986); A renaissance of empiricism, in Tymoczko, T. (Ed.); New Directions in the Philosophy of Mathematics, p.29-48, Birkhauser: Boston, USA.

Lerman, S. (1994); Cultural Perspectives on the Mathematics Classroom, Kluwer Academic Press: Dordrecht, the Netherlands.

Leron, U. (1983); Structuring mathematical proofs, in the American Mathematical Monthly 90, 3, p.174-185.

Leron, U. (1985); A direct approach to indirect proofs, in Educational Studies in Mathematics 16, p.321-325, D. Reidel Publishing Company: Dordrecht, the Netherlands.

Luchins, A. S., and Luchins, E. H. (1965); Logical Foundations of Mathematics for Behavioral Scientists, Holt, Rinehart and Winston: New York, USA.

Lunkenbein, D. (1983); Mental structural images characterizing van Hiele levels of thinking, in the Proceedings of the 5th Conference of the North-American Chapter on the Psychology of Mathematics Education, p.255-262.

Macdonald, I. D. (1978); Insight and intuition in mathematics; in Educational Studies in Mathematics 9, p.411-420, D. Reidel Publishing Company: Dordrecht, the Netherlands.

Manin, Y. (1977); A Course in Mathematical Logic, Springer-Verlag: New York, USA.

Mannoury, G. (1931); Woord en Gedachte, Nordhoff: Groningen, the Netherlands.

Marshall, C. and Rossman, G. B. (1995): Designing Qualitative Research, 2nd edition, Sage Publications: Thousand Oaks, USA.

Martin, W. G. and Harel, G. (1989); Proof frames of preservice elementary teachers, in the Journal for Research in Mathematics Education 20, 1, p.41-51.

Mason, J. (1980); When is a symbol symbolic? in For the Learning of Mathematics 1(2), p.8-12, FLM Publishing association: Montreal, Canada.

Mason, J. (1994); Researching from the inside in mathematics education - locating an I-you relationship, in the Proceedings of the 18th Conference of the International Group for the Psychology of Mathematics Education, Vol. I, p. 176-194, Portugal, Lisbon.

Mason, J. and Pimm, D. (1984); Generic examples: seeing the general in the particular; in Educational Studies in Mathematics 15, p.277-289, D. Reidel Publishing Company: Dordrecht, the Netherlands.

Mason, J., Burton, L. and Stacey, K. (1982); Thinking Mathematically, Addison Wesley: London, UK.

Moore, G. H. (1990); Proof and the infinite, in Interchange 21 1, p.46-60, the Ontario Institute for Studies in Education: Ontario, Canada.

Moore, R. C. (1994); Making the transition to formal proof, in Educational Studies in Mathematics 27, p.249-266, Kluwer Academic Publishers: Dordrecht, the Netherlands.

Movshovits-Hadar, N. (1988a); Stimulating presentation of theorems followed by responsive proofs, in For the Learning of Mathematics 8, 2, p.12-30, FLM Publishing Association: Montreal, Canada.

Movshovits-Hadar, N. (1988b); School mathematics theorems - an endless source of surprise, in For the Learning of Mathematics 8, 3, p.34-40, FLM Publishing Association: Montreal, Canada.

References

Nagel, E. and Newman, J. R. (1959); Gödel's Proof, Routledge & Kegan Paul: London, UK.

Neubrand, M. (1989); Remarks on the acceptance of proofs: the case of some recently tackled major theorems, in For the Learning of Mathematics 9, 3, FLM Publishing Association: Montreal, Canada.

Odell, L. and Goswami, D. (1982); Writing in a non-academic setting, in Research in the Teaching of English 16, 3, p.201-224.

Open University (1988); Project Mathematics Update: Approaching Infinity, Open University: PM752C., Milton Keynes, UK.

Orton, R. E. (1988); Two theories of "theory" in mathematics education: using Kuhn and Lakatos to examine four foundational issues, in For the Learning of Mathematics 8, 2, p.36-43, FLM Publishing Association: Montreal, Canada.

Otte, M. (1990); Intuition and logic, in For the Learning of Mathematics 10, 2, FLM Publishing association: Montreal, Canada.

Owens, D. T., ed. (1993); Research Ideas for the Classroom: Middle Grades Mathematics, Macmillan: New York, USA.

Patton, M. Q. (1987); How to Use Qualitative Methods in Evaluation, Sage Publications: Newbury Park, USA.

Pimm, D. (1987); Speaking Mathematically, Routledge: London, UK.

Pimm, D. (1990); Is the proof in the practice: the nature of argument, in Mathematics in School 3, p.46-48.

Polya, G. (1957); How to Solve It, Doubleday Anchor: New York, USA.

Polya, G. (1967); Mathematical Discovery: On Understanding, Learning and Teaching Problem Solving, John Wiley and Sons: New York, USA.

Polya, G. (1986); Generalization, Specialization, Analogy, in Tymoczko, T. (Ed.); New Directions in the Philosophy of Mathematics, p.103-124, Birkhauser: Boston, USA.

Porteous, K. (1990); What do children really believe? in Educational Studies in Mathematics 21, p.589-598, Kluwer

Academic Publishers: Dordrecht, the Netherlands.

Reid, D. (1995a); Proving to explain, in the Proceedings of the 19th International Conference on the Psychology of Mathematics Education Vol. 3, p.137-143, Recife, Brazil.

Reid, D. (1995b); The Need to Prove, unpublished doctoral dissertation, the University of Alberta: Edmonton, Alberta, Canada.

Restivo, S. (1992); Mathematics in Society and History, Kluwer Academic Press: Dordrecht, the Netherlands

Restivo, S. (1993); The social life of mathematics, in Restivo, S., Van Bendegam, J. P. and Fisher, R. (eds.); Math Worlds: Philosophical and Social Studies in Mathematics and Mathematics Education, p.247-278, SUNY Press: New York, USA.

Restivo, S. (1994); The social life of mathematics, in Ernest, P. (ed.); Mathematics, Education and Philosophy: an International Perspective, Burgess Science Press: Basingstoke, UK.

Rotman, B. (1987); Signifying Nothing: the Semiotics of Zero, Macmillan Press: Basingstoke, UK.

Rotman, B. (1988); Toward a semiotics of mathematics, in Semiotica 72-1/2, p.1-35, Mouton de Gruyter: Berlin, Germany.

Schoenfeld, A. H. (1985); Mathematical Problem Solving, Academic: London, UK.

Schoenfeld, A. H. (1988); When good teaching leads to bad results: the disasters of "well-taught" mathematics courses, in Educational Psychologist, 23, 2, p.145-166.

Schoenfeld, A. H. (1989): Exploration of students' mathematical beliefs and behavior, in the Journal for Research in Mathematics Education 20, 4, p.338-355.

Sconyers, J. M. (1995); Proof and the middle school mathematics student, in Mathematics Teaching in the Middle School 1, 7, p.516-518, NCTM: Reston, Va. USA.

Semadeni, Z. (1984); Action proofs in primary mathematics teaching and in teacher training; in For the Learning of Mathematics 4, FLM Publishing association: Montreal, Canada.

References

Senk, S. L. (1985); How well do students write geometry proofs? Mathematics Teacher, 78, 6.

Senk, S. L. (1989); Van Hiele levels and achievement in writing geometry proofs, in Journal for Research in Mathematics Education 20, 3, p.309-321, NCTM: USA.

Siu, M. (1993); Proof and pedagogy in Ancient China: examples from Liu Hui's commentary on Jiu Zhang Suan Shu, in Educational Studies in Mathematics 24, p.345-357, Kluwer Academic Publishers: Dordrecht, the Netherlands.

South Bank University (1993); Unit Guide: Mathematical Contexts and Strategies, School of Computing, Information Systems and Mathematics.

Steffe, L. P. (1991); The constructivist teaching experiment: illustrations and implication, in von Glasersfeld, E. (ed.); Radical Constructivism in Mathematics Education, p.177-194, Kluwer Academic Publishers: Dordrect, the Netherlands.

Steffe, L. P., von Glasersfeld, E., Richards, J. and Cobb, P. (1983); Childrens' Counting Types: Philosophy, Theory, and Application, Praeger Scientific, New York, USA.

Steiner, H. G. (1987); Philosophical and epistemological aspects of mathematics and their interaction with theory and practice in mathematics education, in For the Learning of Mathematics 7, 1, p.7-13, FLM Publishing Association: Montreal, Canada.

Tall, D. O. (1979); Cognitive aspects of proof, with special reference to the irrationality of $\sqrt{2}$, in the Proceedings of the 3rd International Conference for the Psychology of Mathematics Education, Warwick.

Tall, D. O. (1992); The Transition to Advanced Mathematical Thinking: Functions, Infinity, Limits & Proof , Coventry: MERC.

Tymoczko, T. (1979); The four-color problem and its philosophical significance, in the Journal of Philosophy 76, p.57-83.

Ulam, S. M. (1976); Adventures of a Mathematician, Charles Scribner's Sons: New York, USA.

van Dormolen, J. (1977); Learning to understand what giving a proof really means, in Educational Studies in Mathematics 8, p.27-34, D. Reidel Publishing Company: Dordrecht, the Netherlands.

van Hiele, P. M. (1976); Wie kann man in Mathematikunterricht den Denkstufen rechnung tragen? in Educational Studies in Mathematics 7, p.157-169, D. Reidel Publishing Company: Dordrecht, the Netherlands.

Walther, G. (1984); Communications: Action proof vs illuminating examples? in For the Learning of Mathematics 4, 3, p.10-11, FLM Publishing association: Montreal, Canada.

Wilson, P. S., ed. (1993); Research Ideas for the Classroom: High School Mathematics, Macmillan: New York, USA.

Winbourne, P. and Finlow-Bates, K. (1994); Unit Guide: Mathematical Contexts and Strategies, South Bank University, School of Computing, Information Systems and Mathematics: London, UK.

INDEX

Ingram Content Group UK Ltd.
Milton Keynes UK
UKHW010607020523
421079UK00001B/16

—